M. L.

DROPPING BACK IN

Also by Miriam Hecht and Lillian Traub

Alternatives to College

DROPPING BACK IN

How to Complete Your College Education Quickly & Economically

Miriam Hecht & Lillian Traub

Foreword by Fred M. Hechinger

E. P. DUTTON, INC. • New York

To the hundreds of adult students we've met and talked with, and the millions they represent. Their strength, determination, and sheer learning power have changed the face of American higher education.

Published in the United States by
E.P. Dutton, Inc.,
2 Park Avenue,
New York, N.Y. 10016

Library of Congress Catalog Card Number: 82-70895

ISBN: 0-525-93229-1 (cloth)   0-525-93228-3 (paper)

Published simultaneously in Canada by
Clarke, Irwin & Company Limited,
Toronto and Vancouver

Designed by Nicola Mazzella

10 9 8 7 6 5 4 3 2 1

First Edition

Contents

Foreword

Adult education used to be viewed as something like entertainment. Not any more. College used to be viewed as a place for postadolescents. Not any more. The world has changed, and so has education's mission. Lifelong learning was once a cliché for commencement speeches. Today, it is a necessity for growing numbers of people.

The reasons for these changes are varied and often highly individual. The changes in the aspirations of, and opportunities for, women are an example. Many women in their forties and fifties, who are part of a generation that did not encourage girls to seek careers, want to make up for lost time and prepare to enter the job market. Other women who gave up college, either altogether or in midstream, when they married, want to complete their academic work after their children have grown.

Both men and women today opt more frequently for career changes. They need to retool. The marketplace itself is far less constant. Old activities become obsolete; new ones beckon. The fast-moving worlds of electronics and computers are examples. Automation eliminates entire lines of employment and opens new ones.

For many, a shorter workweek or day and the trend toward earlier retirement present a choice between boredom or striking out in new directions, retraining hands and mind for talents and potential that had been overlooked or neglected.

Whatever the reasons, continuing education has become a major part of American life, and it is certain to grow. The capacity of students past the traditional college age to function well on the campus was first proven—against some strongly expressed doubts by many academic traditionalists—when millions of veterans flocked to the colleges after World War II under the terms of the G.I. Bill of Rights. They not only did well for themselves they brought a new vitality and sense of purpose to the campuses and thus helped the younger students as well.

In my own occasional college teaching, my most memorable and gratifying experience was the teaching of adults: their dedication to learning and the experience they brought with them. I shall never forget the special meaning given to a seminar on the politics of education by the fact that a radical feminist and a veteran police officer faced each other across the table and were able to test their often clashing ideas against each other. The students ranged from their mid-twenties to their late sixties, but they all shared the desire to learn and to complete degrees that their children had long since attained. One of my students was an elderly blind man who recorded the discussions and never came to class unprepared, never missed an assignment.

As adults are, in the terms of this book, dropping in to the nation's colleges in ever growing numbers, they need help. The world of higher education is often set in its ways. It is used to dealing with "college kids" in the fashion of treating young people barely out of their teens; at the same time the college scene is itself in a state of flux, as the enrollment of traditional students declines. Both factors—the inherent academic traditionalism and the trauma of changes imposed by outside forces—make it more difficult for newcomers to find their way.

This is particularly true for older arrivals who are some, and perhaps even many, years removed from formal classroom attendance and who may never have had any college experience. If their knowledge of campus life stems mainly from the image presented by movies and television, they need to correct their perceptions to deal with reality, especially the more sober reality of the contemporary college. Moreover, the adult learner usually comes with less time to waste and a more clear-cut goal. These newcomers need all the help and guidance they can get; more, in fact, than they are likely to find awaiting them in typical administration buildings.

This is precisely the kind of help and guidance the authors of *Dropping Back In: How to Complete Your College Education Quickly and Economically* offer this new breed of students. They know that the mixed band of adult collegiates comes from many different starting points but without the preparation and orientation that have been pounded into traditional freshmen by their high school teachers and guidance counselors. The adult students may be at least as smart and they are certainly more mature; but they are not conditioned to deal with the very special world of the campus. And even if they attended college, some years ago, they need to be brought up-to-date.

As adults constitute a growing segment of the higher education enrollment, increasing numbers of entrepreneurs will zero in on this important market in an effort to make a fast buck. Fly-by-night institutions will offer all kinds of incentives, promising quick and easy degrees, in order to lure adults into their worthless diploma mills. Thus, there is special need for hard data on how to distinguish real degree programs from phony ones; how to tell whether a program, a school or a college is accredited; how to avoid being exploited.

Even between honest degrees there can be a substantial difference in quality and prestige. In addition, many reputable colleges today recognize the value of real-life experience and offer credits for it, without in any way cheapening the degree. Adults will have to be able to distinguish between what is legitimate and what is not.

Those who are familiar with the campus world of two or three decades ago will be surprised by important changes that may affect their newly begun academic careers. For example, there are highly reputable nontraditional ways of earning credits or even a full degree. In some instances, the student may be able to do much, or even most, of the work independently at home, with only occasional meetings with a tutor or mentor. In other instances, credit courses may be taken by television in combination with registration at an accredited nearby campus, which will also administer the examinations and in the end provide the credits and offer the diploma.

The point of all this is that there are far greater varieties of ways in which adults today may pursue their collegiate careers and satisfy their requirements. This is important because adult students' time is obviously more precious and, if they are working while studying, more difficult to fit into the traditional academic schedule. This means that the time must be invested in ways that eliminate waste.

This is, of course, also true of the content of their courses and of the general game plan that is intended to lead them on the most direct route to the desired end: a degree, some specific knowledge, or the beginning of a new career. In contrast to postadolescent undergraduates, adult learners usually cannot afford to take a leisurely academic stroll in the hope of eventually finding themselves on the right path. They already know where they want to go. What they need is reliable and expert advice on how to get there.

This book offers them a road map through the mysterious byways of academia, including some of the deplorable but nevertheless still very substantial red tape. It deals with the fundamental questions of the kind of courses that point to certain career goals. It discusses questions of financing. It explains the mysteries of college catalogs. It tries to make tests and examinations comprehensible to those who have not had to face such hurdles for quite some time, and it takes the terror out of them to the extent that is possible at any age. It deals honestly with the issue of basic skills, which are essential to mature students, too. And it provides guidelines to the questions that concern all students, young and old: how to study, how to move most surefootedly toward the ultimate goal of graduation.

The authors make it clear that dropping back in to college—for the first time or for a return visit—need not be a one-shot affair. Continuing education has no end. It is truly lifelong for those who wish it to be so. But it is the first round that requires special attention and encouragement.

The authors conclude that the most remarkable thing about dropping back in is that it is no longer remarkable. The newspapers still occasionally present wide-eyed reports about a grandmother earning her degree in the same class with her granddaughter, and readers nod their heads in admiration and mild disbelief. But in the years ahead, such events will become less and less remarkable and more and more routine and natural. The time may not be far off when it will be considered more worthy of note that an adult does not continue his or her education.

For the time being, those who continue their education as adults still constitute a minority, though a growing one. And for minorities, life is never simple. This applies to the adult drop ins as well. They will face, as the authors make clear, the difficulties of timing; the double demands of a job and classes, or of dealing with a sick child or a business crisis in the midst of examination time. They will face stiff academic demands in areas, such as mathematics, that are only a vague recollection, or less, from long-past schooldays.

They will, in short, find that the course they have chosen is not without rocky stretches and difficulties. But for increasing numbers it is a worthwhile journey, and for many an essential one. The purpose of this book is to make the difficult possible and to avoid the pitfalls. The authors believe rightly that dropping back in is the wave of the future and that—with the proper help, guidance, and encouragement—satisfaction, joy, and rewards await those who take the plunge.

FRED M. HECHINGER

Acknowledgments

Returning adult students are a top priority in American education. Perhaps this is why we could turn to so many individuals for suggestions and guidance.

Mark Alan Siegel, member of the New York State Assembly and head of its Higher Education Committee, was endlessly helpful in furnishing materials and information as we needed them. His generosity has made our work very much easier.

Every book on higher education reflects the scholarship, insight, and sheer energy of K. Patricia Cross. More than any other person, she has opened the doors of American colleges to returning adults. We have drawn abundantly upon her work and were encouraged by her interest.

Encouragement has also been provided by Fred Hechinger of *The New York Times* and Ursula Schwerin, herself a dropout who returned to become president of New York City Technical College.

For their help in answering questions and providing material, we welcome the opportunity to thank Carol Aslanian of The College Board, Kathleen Beecham of the Council for the Advancement of Experiential Learning (CAEL), Frances S. Berry of the Council of State Governments, Kathy Dinaberg of the University Without

Walls, and Maier Goldberg, chief academic officer of Local 144, a leading labor union for health-related professions.

We are grateful to librarians coast to coast, and in particular to those of the University of California at La Jolla, the San Diego State University, and New York's Mid-Manhattan Library.

Within the City University of New York (CUNY) we drew upon the expertise of so many people, we can mention only a handful. The CUNY Instructional Resource Center, under Dean Marie Lederman, was generous in allowing us the use of its resources and library. Elaine Egues of the CUNY Baccalaureate Program provided her own special insight into the excitement of working with returning adults. At Hunter College we are indebted to Vanessa Farrell of the Veterans' Office, John Irving of the Office of Academic Advising, Gerard Savage of the School of General Studies, Nancy Stevens and Paula Wicklow of Career Counselling, registrar Ruth Weisgal, and Julie Brand, our resident computer expert. Here, too, we must thank the entire library staff and in particular Arthur Goldzweig, Donna Hill, Milton Mittelman, and Earl Shaffer.

We are grateful to the faculty of Teachers College, Columbia University, for first instilling an interest in adult higher education. We owe a special debt to Professors Joel Davitz, Douglas Sloan, and Bruce Vogeli.

The suggestion for this book first came from Marian Skedgell, formerly of E.P. Dutton. Without her imagination, patience, and confidence, it could not have been written.

But above all, we are indebted to the many returning adult students who have shared their experiences with us. We have sketched in a few circumstances of their return to college, but we cannot possibly do full justice to their wisdom, commitment, and enthusiasm. It was they who opened our eyes to the joys of dropping back in.

One

Everybody's Doing It

Historically, the span of human life has been chopped up into slices like a great salami, with each section having a special flavor all its own. First there was the thin slice of early childhood . . . Then came a thicker slice—twelve to twenty years, perhaps—devoted almost exclusively to full-time learning. Next, we had the still thicker chunk of full-time work . . . And finally, came retirement. In this traditional life cycle of the past, the stages of existence were kept rigidly apart.

Ernest L. Boyer,
President, Carnegie Foundation
for the Advancement
of Teaching

Over the last ten years a revolution has taken place in American colleges. Adults—people in their twenties, thirties, forties, and beyond—are turning their backs on this "salami" style of life. Instead, they are combining college with jobs, travel, child rearing, community services, and a hundred other activities and doing all of it vastly better as a result. Today an estimated 5 to 6 million American adults are taking college courses for credit, and the number is growing every day. According to the U.S. Census Bureau, they constitute one-third of all students attending college. About 57 percent are women; 30 percent are black. The great majority are going to school part time. A whopping 72 percent have had some college experience and are coming back to finish up the requirements for a degree.

Perhaps you stayed in college for only a single semester, maybe less. It doesn't matter. Whatever your age, sex, background, motivation, finances, or goals, chances are that someone very much like you is working for a college degree right now.

Take Robert. At nineteen Robert found a job with an import-export firm, chiefly because he spoke Spanish and had a good head for numbers. Now, ten years and two children later, he's working toward a degree in economics. "Sure I'm smart," he'll tell you, "but to keep moving in this business I've got to be a lot smarter." So far, he has earned thirty-eight credits, including three for a television course in accounting and six for passing a first-year Spanish test. Tuition is a problem, but it's not stopping him; he expects college to be the best investment he ever made.

Harold is doing it differently. In 1971, as an eighteen-year-old freshman, he was caught up in the issues of the day: ecology, minority rights, Vietnam, drugs. Classes seemed irrelevant, and after a while he stopped going. Since then, he has supported himself by restaurant work; after hours he has been reading, talking, even signing up for a course or two. Harold is still ready to take on the world, but he recognizes that it calls for more than good intentions. Last year he returned to college as a political science major. Still something of a loner, he chose a school specializing in contract learning; every unit of study is outlined, reviewed with an adviser, and carried out independently. Harold is not sure when he will finish, but he doesn't much care. What he's doing makes sense, not only for himself, but for the society he hoped to salvage a decade ago.

Linda has her own problem. She quit college after two years to become a programming trainee; now she has a promising career in computers. But to move ahead she needs a bachelor's degree. So Linda is ripping into that degree like a bulldozer. She comparison-shopped among colleges, choosing one that gave her full credit for her two years' study. Then she picked up twelve credits for her background in computer science, and another nine by passing examinations in history, trigonometry, and English composition. An extensive computer program, written on the job, did double duty as an independent study project: six more credits. She even requested four credits in photography, based on a portfolio of her work; they allowed her two. Some on-campus evening courses are rounding out the package; by June her degree, and her promotion, should be in the bag.

If Linda is in a hurry, Arlene is at the opposite pole. Weekdays, she's Mrs. James Carlson, keeping house and looking after their three-year-old twins. But on Saturdays Jim takes over while she heads for her weekend college program. Ultimately she hopes to major in nutrition, but meanwhile she's getting the basic requirements out of the way: three hours each of precalculus and English literature. Someday, when the twins are in school, she'll consider a more concentrated program, but for the present her Saturday classes are exactly right.

Thelma never goes to class; an accident some years ago left her essentially homebound. Her field is languages, including a few tough ones like Portuguese and Russian. Her goal is to earn a living as a translator. She works exclusively through television, audiotape, and written materials. College regulations require her to take final examinations under supervision, but if she can't make it to campus, an authorized proctor will come to her.

Cliff, whose income as a printing salesman puts him in the top 2 percent of the country, has his own reasons for attending college. "After two years and a million warnings, they threw me out of parochial school. My mother cried like it was the end of the world. Sure I was carrying on—but Jesus, what's a fifteen-year-old supposed to know?" Cliff's uncle found him a job in a printshop and after that he was on his own. Over the years he acquired a family, a tidy cash reserve, and a high school equivalency diploma. On his eighth wedding anniversary he received a bachelor's degree in psychology. "My folks can't get over it," he boasts, "and believe me, I'm not done yet."

Not all returning adults follow such unconventional patterns. Marie, who is taking a degree in ophthalmic dispensing, finds all the classes she needs in the evening program of a local community college. Victor, after discovering that teaching high school English

does not pay him a living wage, is switching to teaching the handicapped; all the necessary courses are offered in summer school.
And Claire, a biology major with three teen-agers, has chosen a
completely traditional day-session program; her one concession to
her family is to carry twelve credits a semester instead of the usual
fifteen.

Then there's Yvonne. When Yvonne moved to the city what
she missed most was the use of a car. When she saw that darling
double-parked red compact with the keys dangling in the ignition,
how could she resist? What Yvonne didn't appreciate was that le-
gally there's no such thing as "borrowing" a stranger's car; the
word is *stealing,* and the penalty is fourteen months in jail. Nevertheless some good is coming out of it. A nearby college sponsors
classes in the prison, and Yvonne is working toward an associate's
degree in word processing, where salaries are high. Once she gets
out she can save up for her own darling compact—and you can bet
she won't leave the keys in the ignition!

These are some of the people who are revolutionizing college
education. They don't come across like revolutionaries; they're just
ordinary people, going about their business. The only difference is
that their business—and that of millions of others like them—includes getting a college degree.

The old nursery rhyme mentions "butcher, baker, candlestick
maker"; a 1980s update might read "climatologist, caseworker, environmental safety administrator." In today's technological age, it
takes more than goodwill and a strong back to get a job; it takes
specialized, sophisticated skills. Thirty years ago a good cook could
open a restaurant and hope for the best; today a restaurateur studies food control, public relations, dietetics, and interior design.
Business people, who formerly operated on common sense,
shrewdness, and a sense of the market, now need a background in
merchandising and statistical analysis. Nurses use instruments of a
complexity undreamed of a decade ago; stockroom personnel must
handle electronic inventory systems. Even fledgling actors have a
better chance if they understand electricity well enough to lend a
hand with the stage lights. Everywhere we look adults are engaged
in a process of continuing training.

Although some returning students want to advance in their
present careers, others have an eye on entirely new fields. Jorge

prepared to be a concert pianist, but after adding up his first five years' earnings, he is beginning to think that computer science looks good. Marsha makes ends meet as a math teacher, but her idea of the good life includes a penthouse suite with a Picasso over the couch, so she is studying investment banking. And Catherine, who is doing fine as a travel agent, is nonetheless going after a B.S. in geology. "Travel is touchy," she explains. "It's the first thing to be eliminated when times are bad. And if there's a war, or even a few rumblings, forget it! Geology is my safety net—just in case." A 1980 report estimated that 30 million people over the age of twenty-five were studying to prepare for job or career changes.

Research confirms that although the coming decade may not offer the job opportunities of the 1960s and 1970s, there are still jobs to be found. But getting these jobs entails extra planning, study, and training in any of a hundred specialized fields: mathematics, psychology, management, laboratory techniques, public relations, economics, computers, technologies of every kind. Often the bachelor's degree itself is only a stepping-stone to several years of essential graduate work. In a national survey of adults interested in returning to school, 43 percent—close to half—were primarily interested in studies with a job-oriented slant.

At the same time, we cannot overlook the enormous sense of pride and triumph that comes with getting a degree. Janey, who raised two children during the eight years it took her to earn a B.S. in nursing, claims that the only thing that kept her going was the money her new career would bring. Yet when she walked across the stage on graduation day while the children stood on their seats to get a better view, she was closer to crying than she cares to admit. Cliff, the printing salesman mentioned earlier, claims that his bachelor's degree meant more to him than landing a $2 million contract—which he did the same month. Younger graduates tend to perceive the degree as routine, but for adults it is a tremendous personal victory.

The forces that are bringing adults back to college in the 1980s were operating ten, twenty, even fifty years ago. What makes the picture different today?

To answer this question we must look at the colleges themselves. There the answer is obvious. Colleges are reaching out to adult students because the traditional market of eighteen- to twenty-two-year-olds is drying up.

To those of us who remember the college admissions crush of the 1960s and 1970s, this may come as a surprise. But today's numbers tell another story. Fred E. Crossland of the Ford Foundation, discussing the recent decline in college attendance, writes:

> The basic cause is the birthrate decline that started nearly twenty years ago. We know that the largest number of eighteen year olds in American history reached that age in 1979. The numbers are going down and will reach bottom in 1994.

Crossland predicts that by that year, there will be 26 percent fewer eighteen-year-olds than in 1979. Describing the impact on college attendance, he writes:

> There will be a 1 to 2 percent annual fall-off starting in 1982 and continuing until at least the mid-1990s. That means headcount declines in the range of 150,000 to 175,000 annually; the bottoming out in 1995 or 1996 probably will be 1,750,000 to 2,000,000 fewer students than the nearly 12,000,000 in 1981.

Very bluntly, this means that our colleges and universities— many of which have overexpanded in the last two decades—will go hungry over the next fifteen years if they cannot fill thousands, even millions, of empty seats. We are not saying that Harvard or MIT will go begging for students, but if such schools continue to fill up, the pool of applicants for less prominent institutions will be reduced even further. In short, the colleges need *you*.

Every week, the prestigious *Chronicle of Higher Education* announces conferences on student recruitment and retention, or on the learning needs of adults. Colleges, like doctors, lawyers, and other professionals, are just beginning to advertise. They want to maintain their status; they want no blemish on their integrity—but, oh, how they could use the business!

Of course, there is another side to this coin. Many, perhaps most, educators are genuinely sensitive to the special needs of adult students. The first degree program exclusively for adults was offered by New York's Brooklyn College in the 1950s, long before the current enrollment problem. Business and industry also have a stake in the outcome: they demand trained employees to match their technological advances and do not hesitate to operate schools of their own when outside training is not available. Government funding—not enough, but some—has been provided.

Moreover, the students themselves are their best advertisement. Members of the faculty marvel at their determination and self-discipline and often exchange good-natured gossip about their performance.

> "Denise is in my calculus class this term."
> "Really? She couldn't solve the simplest equation when she began two years ago."

> "I see Barney has a column in the school paper. I lost touch with him after he finished my basic composition course."

> "That was Eloise Jones. I helped her with law school applications, and she stopped by to tell me she got in!"
> "How will she manage, with three kids?"
> "Oh, she says it's no problem. They're all in school now."

On many campuses where recent high school graduates arrive with minimal preparation for college-level work, the instructors vie for the evening classes, where returning adults predominate. A recent comparison of older and younger undergraduates reports that

> older undergraduates have stronger capabilities, as opposed to younger undergraduates, for conducting theoretical analytical inquiry, for assuming self-discipline and responsibility for learning activities, for involvement in self-directed tutorial and independent study activities, and for integrating and synthesizing of theoretical materials.

It is an axiom of merchandising that if you want your product to sell you must provide something that people want to buy. This is as true of education as of anything else. You have probably seen ads like the following from a recent Education Supplement to *The New York Times:*

> ... students over the age of 21 can earn a degree with other adults. Credit is available for prior learning and for life

experience as well. Classes are conveniently scheduled to meet the requirements of adults with responsibilities. And are held in over 21 convenient locations. (New York)

. . . an unusual and exciting way to complete your degree without leaving your job or your present location. Individualized curriculum planning. Study at your own pace. Credit awarded for past qualified work and life experience. (Washington, D.C.)

Earn a degree without entering a classroom. Women's External Degree Program. (Indiana)

Independent Study Program. Design your own program through carefully supervised study at your location. Meet periodically with your team to monitor progress and help design further inquiry. (Massachusetts)

It's about time a college education was designed to meet your needs. The —— College external degree; a flexible, academically excellent program that allows you to earn a B.A., B.S., or B.F.A. degree in one of ten majors and spend only a single weekend on campus each semester. (New Jersey)

You may now opt for off-campus degree/Law Programs. Work toward B.S., M.S., M.B.A., Ph.D., J.D. Weekend Bachelor's Challenge Examination. (California)

The message is unmistakable. When higher education was a sellers' market, it came predominantly in one model: four years, full time, on the heels of graduation from high school. Today it is offered in a hundred shapes, sizes, and varieties.

However, these new, nontraditional programs raise questions of their own. First, unless you have been keeping abreast of academic jargon, you may not know what they are talking about. Second, the programs may not be right for you in any event. Third, and most serious, the courses, the credits, and the degrees offered through some of these programs may not live up to your expectations. You want your courses to be comparable to those offered elsewhere and your credits to be transferable to other schools. You want to be considered eligible for federal or state financial aid. Above all, you want your degree to be acceptable for purposes of employment, civil service eligibility, licensing, and admission to graduate school. Some of the advertised programs meet these requirements; others do not.

Not that the ads are lying; they tell the truth. Unfortunately, many readers, unfamiliar with the ins and outs of college administration, do not know how to interpret the truth. They accept the word *accredited* without asking, "Accredited by whom?" They sign up for professional programs that do not meet the standards of the appropriate licensing agency. (Such programs may be offered even by accredited schools!) If you ask what these readers mean by the word *college*, they will say simply that it's where you study after you graduate from high school.

There's a lot more to college than that.

Two

Colleges, Credits, and Degrees

What is a college?

Sara thought she knew when, two years after graduation from high school, she enrolled at the X Business College. The school was convenient, and the friendly staff readily persuaded her that studying office skills along with beginning college subjects was a sound idea. A year later, with thirty credits on her transcript, Sara decided to transfer to the state university as an accounting major. Only then did she discover that none of her work was acceptable. Despite its name, the X Business College was not an accredited institution.

Every year, thousands of students find themselves in the same boat. After making their plans and investing time and money, they discover, as Sara did, that they are no closer to a degree than when they began.

What does it mean to say that a college is, or is not accredited? The word *college* by itself is no guarantee. Check your telephone directory; unless it's forbidden by law, you'll find barbering colleges, business colleges, colleges of automotive repair, religious studies, and a dozen other fields. Yet when we talk of earning college credit and getting a college degree, such schools are not what we have in mind. We are thinking of a recognized, bona fide college with the right to grant a "real" degree.

In the United States, college and university accrediting is the responsibility of six regional associations, each covering a specific part of the country. These six associations are:

Middle States Association of Colleges and Secondary Schools: Canal Zone, Delaware, District of Columbia, Maryland, New Jersey, New York, Pennsylvania, Puerto Rico, Virgin Islands.

New England Association of Schools and Colleges: Connecticut, Maine, Massachusetts, New Hampshire, Rhode Island, Vermont.

North Central Association of Colleges and Secondary Schools: Arizona, Arkansas, Colorado, Illinois, Indiana, Iowa, Kansas, Michigan, Minnesota, Missouri, Nebraska, New Mexico, North Dakota, Ohio, Oklahoma, South Dakota, West Virginia, Wisconsin, Wyoming.

Northwest Association of Secondary and Higher Schools: Alaska, Idaho, Montana, Nevada, Oregon, Utah, Washington.

Southern Association of Colleges and Schools: Alabama, Florida, Georgia, Kentucky, Louisiana, Mississippi, North Carolina, South Carolina, Tennessee, Texas, Virginia.

Western Association of Schools and Colleges: American Samoa, California, Guam, Hawaii, Trust Territory of the Pacific.

When a college opens, it may spend several years developing programs, recruiting students and staff, and so on. Then, if it wants to become accredited, it contacts the appropriate regional association. At this point it has "requested accreditation." In practice, all this means is that a letter has been sent out. It says absolutely nothing about the school's qualifications or ultimate acceptance. Schools can, and do, request accreditation for appearance sake, even when they know they do not stand a chance of getting it.

At the regional association's end the request sets in motion a good deal of research to establish that the college is responsible and well intentioned. If the school survives this screening—which may take several years—it is given *correspondent* status. Again, this signifies nothing about ultimate accreditation.

Now the process begins in earnest. There are visits, reports, correspondence, meetings, negotiations—and then return visits, revised reports, and so on. Of particular interest are the school's libraries and laboratories, its courses of study, its financial stability, the qualifications of its faculty, and its plans for the future. Typically, the process takes several years. Then, if all goes well, the college officially becomes a *candidate for accreditation*. Translated, this means, "You look good so far, but let's not rush into anything. We'll be watching you for a while longer." In fact, most colleges accepted as candidates for accreditation usually receive it, but the procedure can take another five years or more.

Once a college becomes regionally accredited, its courses and degrees are accepted throughout the country. After that the regional association pays a return visit every ten years or so to make sure standards are being maintained, and more often if there appear to be any problems or important changes. This is no mere formality. Colleges that have fallen below association standards have been known to lose their accreditation, which usually means going out of business.

We have been talking about *regional accreditation*. Do not confuse it with the shorter term, *accreditation*. Plain accreditation can come from a number of agencies and has a variety of meanings. Professional groups like the American Dietetics Association and the National League for Nursing approve specific programs—*not* entire colleges—within their fields. In addition, each state spells out its own licensing requirements in fields related to public health and welfare; these are critically important if you are considering such a field. Some states may also "accredit" schools within their borders, but this is little more than a license to do business, just as a supermarket or a hardware store needs a license. A business organization, the Cosmetology Accrediting Commission, inspects and approves beauty schools, but this means only that they are above-average beauty schools; it cannot turn them into colleges. There also are organizations that have been created for the sole purpose of accrediting schools that could never achieve it otherwise. Often the names of these groups are deliberately misleading and easily confused with those of legitimate organizations.

For our purposes, accredited *will mean* regionally accredited *unless stated otherwise. This in turn means accreditation by one of the six official groups listed on page 11.*

The question of accreditation is complicated by the fact that there are a number of exciting new nonaccredited schools. The Union for Experimenting Colleges and Universities, which coordinates thirty-one University Without Walls programs throughout the United States, is at present only a candidate for accreditation. International College in Los Angeles, featuring individual study with such figures as Buckminster Fuller, Yehudi Menuhin, and Ravi Shankar, is still unaccredited, although its degrees have been recognized by thirty-nine graduate schools including Harvard and Johns Hopkins. Many excellent art and music schools are too specialized to be accredited; they provide first-rate instruction in their fields and do not claim to do anything else. The "people's schools" and "free colleges" that sprang up in the 1970s are deliberately exploring new ways to learn and have no interest in conforming to accreditation standards.

Nonetheless, if you are looking for recognized college credit leading to a recognized college degree, attending a nonaccredited school means taking a chance. Your degree from a nonaccredited college could be turned down by graduate schools, licensing agencies, or prospective employers. Your course work may not be recognized outside the school itself. You may not even be in line for veterans' benefits or financial aid.

There are several thousand accredited colleges and universities across the country. They offer a vast variety of programs; tuition can vary from over $6,000 a year to nothing at all. There are plenty to choose from. Unless you have a compelling reason for attending a nonaccredited school, stick to those that are regionally accredited. Even if you think you have a compelling reason, talk it over with an impartial adviser before making up your mind.

Any discussion of colleges must touch on the subject of credit. Credits are the usual system by which the college recognizes your achievements as a student. One credit represents one hour a week of classes for a semester (usually about fourteen weeks), backed up by two hours a week of outside study. A typical one-semester "major" course like English or psychology will meet for three hours a week and carry three credits. On the other hand, a three-hour swimming course may carry only one credit because there are no outside assignments.

When the credit system was first introduced early in the twentieth century, it was felt that full-time students should work as hard as any other group. At that time the typical work week was forty-eight hours. Translated into college study, this meant that the "traditional" load for full-time students with no outside responsibilities was fixed at about fifteen credits per semester, representing that many hours a week of classes plus thirty hours a week of assignments. Today, less than one quarter of entering students complete college at this rate. Nonetheless, you are considered to be in your "first" or "freshman" year until you have earned thirty credits—no matter how long you've been working at it. Similarly, your "second" year is the period between thirty and sixty credits, and so on.

Apart from their credit-bearing courses, many colleges offer extension or continuing education courses. Very often, these courses—which may be anything from folk dancing to ancient Greek—have no required assignments, examinations, or papers, and carry no credit. These are the courses for which adults sign up when they have no interest in a degree and want to study just for fun. Even if the extension course is identical with one offered in the regular curriculum, the regular course will receive credit whereas the extension version may not. The reason is that although students can learn a great deal in extension courses, they are never called on to prove it. No proof, no credit; it's as simple as that. So if there is any chance that you will ever want college credit for any purpose at all, you should avoid no-credit extension courses.

If you accumulate enough credits, maintain a C average or better, and satisfy college requirements about the content and distribution of your courses, you will find yourself in line for a degree. Colleges and degrees go hand in hand. Colleges are unique in their authority to grant degrees; degrees are important because they tell the world that you have been successful at college-level work.

Degrees can be traced back to the Middle Ages, when each trade or craft was controlled by a guild that set standards and licensed qualified workmen. If this was important in ordinary trades, it was even more so in the professions. Hence the church and state authorized a few outstanding universities to grant degrees, indicating that the recipients were qualified to practice their chosen professions. The degree was a credential, a stamp of approval. It retains that meaning to this day.

When we talk of *the degree*, we are usually referring to the bachelor's degree. This is awarded in the liberal arts (B.A.) or the sciences (B.S.) after completing 120 credits—four years of successful full-time study—in appropriate college-level courses. These courses usually include a block of required introductory subjects, such as expository writing, mathematics, and a foreign language, ten to twelve courses in a major field of study, and at least four in a related minor field. Remaining courses are electives: students may select whatever interests them, as long as they have the necessary background.

In time, it was recognized that 120 credits are too many for some purposes and too few for others. At one end of the scale, associate's degrees were introduced, indicating the completion of 60 credits. These are offered in the community colleges (also known as junior, or two-year, colleges) and are of three types. The Associate in Arts (A.A.) and Associate in Science (A.S.) are like the first half of a bachelor's program; in fact, the recipients often finish up their work in a four-year college. The Associate in Applied Science (A.A.S.) is more career oriented. Students combine a year of liberal arts study with intensive training in such areas as health science, data processing, business, or technology, and go on to jobs in the field.

At the other end of the scale we have graduate degrees—the master's and the doctorate—for study beyond the bachelor's level. The doctorate usually requires ninety additional credits and the master's thirty or more; they may also involve comprehensive examinations, original research, and mastery of at least one foreign language. Graduate work is usually done at a university, which has been described as a "collection of colleges" and provides both graduate and undergraduate study in a wide variety of fields.

Sometimes a student is more interested in specific courses than in a degree. Richard, with an overriding passion for music, is an example. His idea of the perfect program is Harmony, Advanced Ear Training, Composition, Performance IV (in anything from clavichord to drums), and, for a change of pace, History of Music. As he sees it, a college degree will not make any difference in his life. Should he nevertheless complete the degree requirements?

He probably should. Granted, he may be able to take his music courses as a nonmatriculated student, that is, as a student outside the degree program. But from a purely practical point of view, if he goes this route the chances are that he cannot:

> receive certain types of financial aid;
> succeed in getting the courses and teachers he really wants (nonmatriculated students are usually allowed to register only after all the matriculated students have had their turn);
> gain the complete attention and respect of the senior faculty;
> have first claim on practice rooms, instruments, taping equipment, and other resources;
> get into graduate school;
> qualify for jobs which, officially or unofficially, call for a degree;
> persuade his girl friend's parents that he's a solid citizen and not just a music freak;
> enjoy the satisfaction of knowing he's completed one of the more significant projects of his life.

Don't underestimate the importance of a degree. It opens doors and creates opportunities you may not even be aware of. Psychologically, it represents a milestone; mature students often return for a degree simply to prove that they can do it. And for someone like Richard, who is taking college courses anyway, fulfilling degree requirements results in substantial rewards for a relatively small additional effort. As one student put it when she returned to school after ten years and nineteen jobs, "It's better to have a degree and not need it than to need a degree and not have it."

Three

The Breakthrough in Higher Education

Today's new programs in higher education have labels that may confuse you. Northeastern University offers "co-op education." The University Without Walls, where the average undergraduate is close to thirty-five, features "self-paced learning," "community resources," and "contact learning." The New York State Regents External Degree program offers a "fully external degree" with credit for "prior learning." Other programs mention "independent study," "credit for CLEP, CPE, and REDE examinations," "mediated instruction," or "life experience." How can you choose what is best for you when you do not even know the meaning of the words?

Put your mind at rest. Some of these labels refer to innovations as simple as scheduling classes on weekends instead of during the week. Others are as elaborate as having students prepare substantial portfolios to demonstrate that they already know material for which the college is currently granting credit. Virtually all these innovations are particularly valuable for returning students, with their sense of purpose, their outside responsibilities, and their impatience with time-consuming, unnecessary routine. Often these new programs are the best if not the only way to complete your college degree.

WHAT DO YOU WANT TO STUDY?

Until the Civil War, no one ever asked what students wanted to study. The curriculum was the same for virtually everyone, with little variation from student to student and even from college to college. Gradually, options were introduced; in 1980 the *College Blue Book* listed over 2,000 majors leading to a bachelor's degree. Of course, no single campus offers all these majors. Thus, although virtually every liberal arts college has a bachelor's degree in history, the *Blue Book* lists only thirty offering it in urban studies, twenty-six in real estate, and six in audiology.

If you cannot find what you want among these 2,000 fields, many colleges will allow you to design your own interdisciplinary major, choosing courses from two or more areas. Nell, for example, is interested in sports journalism; she planned a major straddling the physical education and communications departments. A stage-craft major may include courses in theater, art, and physics—the last to provide a background in lighting and acoustics. Other fields that lend themselves to interdisciplinary study include international affairs, ecology, third world studies, public health, and linguistics.

What if you are not sure of your major? Most colleges don't expect you to decide until some time in your second year; even then, you are allowed to change your mind. In the meantime, students usually play it safe by registering for staple introductory courses in a variety of fields: for example, expository writing, psychology, or science. No matter what your ultimate major or where you get your degree, you can usually count on receiving some credit for courses like these.

If, after several semesters, you still don't want to pin yourself down, you can consider one of the new B.A. programs in general studies or liberal arts. These programs allow you to explore the entire curriculum in some depth, without concentrating in any one area.

CAN YOU GET CREDIT FOR PRIOR LEARNING?

We have already noted that the system of college credits originated as a measure of time spent in a course. But for returning adults, many of whom have learned a great deal in or out of college, *knowledge*, rather than mere time, is becoming the important criterion. As a reentry student, you can get credit for what you know, regardless of where you learned it or how long it took. If you can demonstrate knowledge of college-level work, you are in line for college credit.

Such credit is of three types: transfer credit, credit by examination, and credit for life experience. Sometimes the term *prior learning* is used to cover all three; sometimes it is used only as a substitute for *life experience*, which has proved to be a misleading term. In any case, many college-bound adults—even those who are enrolling for the first time—are discovering that something in their past can earn them credit today.

The chief source of prior credit is transfer credit from other colleges. Many schools accept such credits routinely, although the courses may count only as electives. Holders of associate degrees have a good chance of being admitted directly into the junior year, particularly if they are transferring from a community college to a senior college in the same municipal or state system. A few schools have no across-the-board policy, preferring to evaluate each student individually. The date of your transfer credit may also be a factor; some colleges draw the line at giving credit for courses taken more than ten or fifteen years ago.

Transfer credit is by no means limited to courses taken on campus. Today, at least 5 million adults are taking classes in connection with their jobs and another 1.5 million through the armed forces. Many of these courses duplicate college work and will qualify for college credit.

The responsibility for reviewing industrial and military courses has been assumed by the American Council on Education (ACE), a national coordinating agency with offices in Washington, D.C. This group has actually examined hundreds of courses, identifying their college-level equivalents and making recommendations on how many credits to allow. A second guide, limited to industry courses, has been prepared by New York State. Sample pages from these volumes appear on pages 20 and 21. For example, the course servicing the loan, collecting amounts due, credit evaluation, and collection policies and procedures); legal aspects; financial statement analysis; credit department management; indirect instalment lending. (Prerequisite: Principles of Bank Operations.)

Credit recommendation: In the lower division baccalaureate/associate degree category or in the upper division baccalaureate category, 3 semester hours in Banking or Finance (6/78).

International Banking

Location: Various area high school and college facilities.
Length: 45 hours (15 weeks).
Dates: June 1968–Present.
Objective: To present the student with the basic framework and fundamentals of international banking, including the transfer of money, the financing of trade, the role of international agencies, the work of commercial banks, and foreign currency transactions.
Instruction: World of international banking; international activities of United States and foreign banks; correspondent banking relationships; foreign exchange; letters of credit; bankers' acceptances; collections; international lending; Euro-dollar market.
Credit recommendation: In the upper division baccalaureate category, 3 semester hours in Banking or Finance (6/78).

Introduction to Computers
(Formerly Fundamentals of Bank Data Processing)

Location: Various area high school and college facilities.
Length: 45 hours (15 weeks).
Dates: June 1968–Present.
Objective: To provide the student with the basic concepts of electronic data processing with special reference to bank automation.
Instruction: Survey of data processing and computer concepts as applied to banks; data recording, processing, and input and output; computer programming (flow charting and coding). A visit is made to a bank data processing center. (Prerequisite: Business Mathematics.)
Credit recommendation: In the lower division baccalaureate/associate degree category, 3 semester hours in Electronic Data Processing (6/78).

Law and Banking

Location: Various area high school and college facilities.
Length: 45 hours (15 weeks).
Dates: January 1976–Present.
Objective: To provide the student with a knowledge of the basic concepts of business law, with emphasis on the Uniform Commercial Code.
Instruction: Court system and civil procedures; contracts; quasi-contracts; property; torts and crimes; agency; partnerships; corporations; sales of personal property; commercial paper and bank deposits/collections; documents of title; secured transactions.

Credit recommendation: In the lower division baccalaureate/associate degree category or in the upper division baccalaureate category, 3 semester hours in Business Administration or Business Law (6/78).

Macroeconomics

Location: Various area high school and college facilities.
Length: 45 hours (15 weeks).
Dates: September 1978–Present.
Objective: To provide the student with a knowledge of the theory and practical application of the basic concepts of macroeconomics.
Instruction: Price system; comparative economic systems; supply, demand, and equilibrium; elasticity of demand; circular flow; inflation; unemployment; national income accounting; aggregate supply and demand; the multiplier; fiscal policy; consumption and investment; business cycles; the Federal Reserve System; money creation; the public sector; economic growth.
Credit recommendation: In the lower division baccalaureate/associate degree category, 3 semester hours in Business Administration or Economics (6/78).

Management Psychology

Location: Various area high school and college facilities.
Length: 45 hours (15 weeks).
Dates: September 1973–Present.
Objective: To provide the student with an understanding of the various organizational factors and procedures that determine career growth and progress.
Instruction: Growth and history of the human relations concept; the supervisor's job; leadership and its effect on employees; motivation and job advancement; training new employees; self-development and development of others; problem solving.
Credit recommendation: In the lower division baccalaureate/associate degree category or in the upper division baccalaureate category, 2 semester hours in Behavioral Science or Business Administration (5/78).

Marketing for Bankers

Location: Various area high school and college facilities.
Length: 45 hours (15 weeks).
Dates: September 1976–Present.
Objective: To provide the student with an understanding and appreciation of the marketing function in banking.
Instruction: Marketing concept; the market and market segmentation; market research; consumer motivation and behavior; consumerism; controlling marketing efforts; product; price; distribution; advertising; promotion; presentations. (Prerequisites: Macroeconomics and Principles of Bank Operations.)
Credit recommendation: In the lower division baccalaureate/associate degree category, 3 semester hours in Business Administration or Marketing (6/78).

A Guide to Educational Programs in Noncollegiate Organizations (Albany, N.Y.: The University of the State of New York, 1980). The courses described here are offered by the American Institute of Banking.

All Versions: 3750th Technical School, Sheppard AFB, TX.

Length: *Version 1:* 8 weeks (228–240 hours). *Version 2:* 8 weeks (240 hours).

Exhibit Dates: *Version 1:* 5/71–12/73. *Version 2:* 2/64–4/71.

Objectives: To train airmen in budgeting, financial planning, and financial management for Air Force personnel.

Instruction: Lectures and practical exercises in the fundamentals of Air Force budgeting, principles and procedures of budget administration, developing estimates of requirements, and preparation of operating budgets and financial plans.

Credit Recommendation: *Version 1:* In the lower-division baccalaureate/associate degree category, 3 semester hours in budgeting and financial administration (2/74); in the upper-division baccalaureate category, 3 semester hours in budgeting and financial administration (2/74). *Version 2:* In the lower-division baccalaureate/associate degree category, 4 semester hours in finance and budget planning (2/74); in the upper-division baccalaureate category, 4 semester hours in finance and budget planning (12/68).

AF-1408-0018

DISBURSING SUPERVISOR

Course Number: AA81170.

Location: 3415th Technical Training Center, Lowry AFB, CO.

Length: 13 weeks (390 hours).

Exhibit Dates: 3/54–12/68.

Objectives: To train enlisted personnel to supervise disbursing activities.

Instruction: Lectures in the duties of a disbursing supervisor. Course includes introduction to disbursing, military pay, travel allowances, commercial accounts, accounting for public funds, and financial office management.

Credit Recommendation: In the lower-division baccalaureate/associate degree category, 3 semester hours in funds disbursement (2/74); in the upper-division baccalaureate category, 4 semester hours in general business practice (12/68).

AF-1408-0019

DISBURSING CLERK

Course Number: AB81130.

Location: 3415th Technical Training Group, Lowry AFB, CO.

Length: 10 weeks (300 hours).

Exhibit Dates: 3/54–12/68.

Objectives: To train enlisted personnel in disbursing and accounting procedures.

Instruction: Lectures in the duties of a disbursing clerk. Course includes introduction to disbursing, military pay, travel allowances, commercial accounts, accounting for public funds, and financial office management.

Credit Recommendation: In the lower-division baccalaureate/associate degree category, 3 semester hours in disbursing finance (2/74); in the upper-division baccalaureate category, 3 semester hours in general business practice (12/68).

AF-1408-0020

HEATING PLANT MANAGEMENT AND SUPERVISION

Course Number: AAN54770-1.

Location: 3750th Technical School, Sheppard AFB, TX.

Length: 4 weeks (108 hours).

Exhibit Dates: 3/67–12/68.

Objectives: To provide skills for the supervision and management of a heating plant.

Instruction: Principles and procedures employed in heating plant supervision and management are taught, including operation and maintenance of common combustion control instruments, heating plant management and combustion principles, boiler water sampling, testing, treatment, scale and corrosion control in steam and high-temperature hot water heating plants and systems, and organizational control, including workload evaluation.

Credit Recommendation: In the lower-division baccalaureate/associate degree category, 2 semester hours in heating plant supervision and management (11/77).

AF-1408-0022

PROFESSIONAL PERSONNEL MANAGEMENT

Course Number: None.

Location: Institute for Professional Development, Maxwell AFB, AL.

Length: 6 weeks (204 hours).

Exhibit Dates: 7/72–Present.

Objectives: To provide senior personnel managers with a better understanding of modern management theory, human behavior, contemporary social issues, and technological skills.

Instruction: Lectures in management environment, management processes, managerial behavioral science, labor relations, information systems, and personnel administration.

Credit Recommendation: In the upper-division baccalaureate category, 6 semester hours in management, 3 in labor relations (2/74).

AF-1408-0023

PERSONNEL SERVICES OFFICER

Course Number: OB7341.

Location: 3310th Technical School, Scott AFB, IL.

Length: 6 weeks (180 hours).

Exhibit Dates: 6/55–12/68.

Objectives: To train officers to manage personnel services activities for Air Force personnel and their dependents.

Instruction: Lectures and laboratories in personnel management, including human relations, vocational and educational guidance, personal affairs activities, character guidance, community services, and dependents education; and the personnel services organization, including funds, supplies, communications, and entertainment and recreational activities and facilities.

Credit Recommendation: In the lower-division baccalaureate/associate degree category, 3 semester hours in personnel administration (2/74); in the upper-division baccalaureate category, 3 semester hours in applied sociology (12/68).

AF-1408-0024

EXECUTIVE ENGINEERING

Course Number: None.

Location: Civil Engineering School, Wright-Patterson AFB, OH.

Length: 3 weeks (115 hours).

Exhibit Dates: 2/73–Present.

Objectives: To provide officers and civilian personnel with advanced training in civil engineering management.

Instruction: Lectures on motivational theory; communication; economics; leadership dynamics and creativity; and organizing, planning, and decision-making techniques.

Credit Recommendation: In the lower-division baccalaureate/associate degree category, 3 semester hours in management (2/74); in the upper-division baccalaureate category, 3 semester hours in management (2/74).

AF-1408-0025

ADVANCED SYSTEMS BUYING

Course Number: 172.

Location: School of Systems and Logistics, Wright-Patterson AFB, OH.

Length: 4 weeks (160 hours).

Exhibit Dates: 1/69–8/73.

Objectives: To teach officers and civilian personnel the basic principles of procurement management.

Instruction: Lectures in the principles of procurement management, including Army project procurement; economics; cost estimating, programming, scheduling, and controlling defense systems procurement; and leadership, decision-making, and communication techniques.

Credit Recommendation: In the lower-division baccalaureate/associate degree category, 2 semester hours in industrial procurement (2/74); in the upper-division baccalaureate category, 2 semester hours in industrial procurement (2/74).

AF-1408-0026

SURVEILLANCE OF PERFORMANCE MEASUREMENT SYSTEMS

Course Number: 195.

Location: School of Systems and Logistics, Wright-Patterson AFB, OH.

Length: 2 weeks (60 hours).

Exhibit Dates: 2/73–Present.

Objectives: To train officers and civilian personnel to perform the maintenance and surveillance of contractor performance-measurement systems.

Instruction: Lectures and discussions on the design and maintenance of a contractor's system, with emphasis on logic, data analysis, data system troubleshooting, and problem analysis; and budgeting and accounting of surveillance systems.

Credit Recommendation: No credit because of the limited specialized nature of the course (2/74).

AF-1408-0027

PHASE II SYSTEMS MANAGEMENT

Course Number: 3OZR5155.

Location: School of Applied Aerospace Sciences, Sheppard AFB, TX.

Length: 2 weeks (60 hours).

Exhibit Dates: 8/72–12/73.

Objectives: To prepare qualified data processing installation managers and machine room supervisors as B 3500 computer operations systems managers.

Instruction: Lectures and practical exercises in B 3500 data processing installation concepts, B 3500 system, B 3500 loaders and utilities, on-line systems management, and management problems.

Guide to the Evaluation of Educational Experiences in the Armed Forces (Washington, D.C.: American Council on Education, 1978).

Law and Banking offered by the American Institute of Banking is worth three semester hours; the air force course AF-1408-0018 for disbursing supervisors is worth four semester hours. While ACE recommendations are taken seriously, individual colleges use their own judgment on whether to allow such credit and how much.

Even without taking courses, you can receive college credit for what you already know by passing tests designed and administered by certain recognized agencies. The best known of these programs is the College-Level Examination Program—CLEP for short. For a fee of about $25, you can take a CLEP test in any of over fifty college subjects, almost anywhere in the world. Other testing programs are offered by the New York State Regents, New Jersey's Thomas Edison College, and the armed forces (for military personnel and certain classes of veterans only). Credit can also be received for advanced-placement exams given in high school, for Graduate Record Examinations (GREs), and for several less common types of test. Over 1,800 colleges accept such tests. Moreover, if you believe you know the content of some college course, you can ask the department to prepare a special "challenge examination" so that you can demonstrate your knowledge and receive credit.

Finally, college credit may be allowed by a review of life experience. This is a sensitive subject. Pace University cautions its prospective students:

> The phrase "life experience" credit is frequently misunderstood; it is not credit given for "experience" *per se*, nor is it credit given for "living." Rather, L.E. credit is awarded for academically valid, college-equivalent, *demonstrable* learning derived from various *non*-college sources. Thus, "life experience" credit may be granted to matriculated students who, through experience, professional certification, self-education, in-service training, adult education or "in-house" courses, or other means outside the formal context of the college classroom, have acquired and can demonstrate knowledge in various fields of study taught at Pace University and other colleges.

Thus, one student's knowledge of German earned her six credits; another's knowledge of Esperanto earned him nothing at all. Susan is a whiz at entertaining: six people or sixty, she carries it off magnificently. But she is not likely to get credit unless she can track down some college course that teaches the same skill.

On the other hand, students find it painful to be told that years of personally significant life experience are worthless in terms of credit. Veterans have demanded credit for having fought in a war, and women have argued that raising a child is equally credit worthy.

Some colleges resolve the problem by granting no credit at all for life experience. Others have a policy of allowing such credit but are very leery of implementing it. The picture is further complicated by the fact that evaluating prior learning takes a long time; most schools will not even undertake it until after you enroll.

Receiving the maximum number of credits for prior learning can save you thousands of dollars and years of valuable time. Because college policies vary enormously from one campus to another, comparing them can easily justify the time required. In chapter 7, you'll find out how to go about it.

CAN YOU MANAGE YOUR OWN INSTRUCTION?

When it comes to the business of learning, the traditional college student is in the hands of the instructors. Not only do they lecture but they determine the content and emphasis of the course, the use of class time, and the criteria by which students are judged. These responsibilities, usually described as *course management*, are even more important than the actual job of lecturing.

For young students, this makes sense. After all, to manage your own instruction, you need the appropriate skills: good motivation and work habits, clearly defined goals, a feeling for the scope of the subject, and a realistic appraisal of your own strengths and weaknesses.

These are precisely the skills that adult learners are apt to have. In *Redefining the Discipline of Adult Education* (1980), Robert D. Boyd and Jerold Apps have noted:

> While some adult learners need help in formulating their learning objectives, in identifying sources of information, and in measuring achievement, many other learners do not need such guidance. These are the autonomous learners. A fully au-

tonomous learner is a person who can identify his learning need when he finds a problem to be solved, a skill to be acquired, or information to be obtained . . . In implementing his need, he gathers the information he desires, collects ideas, practices skills, works to resolve his problems, and achieves his goals.

In short, autonomous adult learners are capable of managing their own learning, and increasingly, they are being allowed to do so.

Often this takes the form of "independent study"—also known by such names as "self-directed study" and "contract learning." The student maps out a project, locates an adviser or "mentor" (not necessarily connected with the college), obtains departmental approval, and gets to work. In contract learning, all of this is written out and signed by student and adviser, hence the name. A sample contract, used by Hunter College in New York City, appears on pages 25 and 26.

Many independent study projects, particularly in the social sciences and performing arts, involve working within the community. Thus, a sociology student earned six credits by supervising the publication of a weekly newsletter in a senior citizens' center. An architecture major joined in the rebuilding of a run-down tenement. A half dozen drama students received four credits apiece for organizing a Spanish-language neighborhood theater group. In cases like these the program may be described as "field study," "community participation," or "applied study experience."

In other fields, independent study may be carried out in the library, the laboratory, or in the comfort of your own home. Mary, at her kitchen table, wrote a collection of short stories. Kenneth conducted a telephone survey of community views on local health services. Whatever your field, the independent study project is an opportunity to manage your own education.

Independent study is more appropriate for advanced students than for beginners. However, even students in introductory courses can sometimes find ways to manage their own learning. These frequently involve the source from which you get the actual information you need—what educators call the *vehicle of instruction.*

The traditional vehicle of instruction is a combination of instructors and books, and both are still in widespread use. However, college courses are now offered via radio, television, tape, computer, and even newspapers and telephones. As these approaches involve the use of audiovisual media, they are referred to, collec-

HUNTER COLLEGE OF THE CITY UNIVERSITY OF NEW YORK
  Office of Academic and Admissions Advising
    695 Park Avenue, New York, N.Y. 10021

                                    Advising - Room 108
                                         570-5205

INDEPENDENT LEARNING BY ACHIEVEMENT CONTRACT PROGRAM

                              DATE_____

            CONTRACT

NAME_____MATRIC_____NON-DEGREE_____
   (first)   (last)

SOC. SEC. #_____ MAJOR/MINOR_____

ADDRESS_____ DAY_____ EVE (SGS)_____

            _____ #CREDITS COMPLETED_____

TELEPHONE #_____ Fall_____Spring_____Summer_____

1) Project proposal is as follows: (explain)

2) Evaluation will be based on: (written paper, classroom exam,
    a performance, a lecture, a laboratory research project, a
    mock trial, etc.)
                      _____

3) Number of credits to be earned: _____

4) Grading option (check one): Letter grade_____ CR/NCR_____

5) Progress reports will be presented in the following manner:

Have your committee sign this contract. Submit a copy to your
evaluation chairperson; you keep a copy; return the original to
Room 108.

COMMITTEE MEMBERS   SIGNATURES   DEPARTMENT

Evaluative Chairperson_____   _____

Faculty Member_____   _____

Faculty Member_____   _____

If project is not completed in one semester as specified above,
I understand that I must follow the College's standard procedure
for extension of INCs.

                              _____
                                 Student's Signature

tively, as *mediated instruction.* But because even the best computer or television course cannot anticipate every difficulty of every student, mediated instruction is usually supplemented by tutors, paraprofessionals, or instructors whom you can contact in moments of crisis.

What leeway does mediated instruction provide in the management of your own learning? In some programs you have the option of working off-campus, possibly at home. Or you can schedule your work at your own convenience. Sometimes the resources for a given course cover a variety of topics from which you can select those that interest you. Occasionally, the course is open-ended; you yourself set the pace and determine how much time you will need. (Such programs are called *self-paced;* by contrast, traditional programs are *instructor-paced.*) Whatever the vehicle of instruction, you will still be expected to complete assignments, write reports, and take supervised examinations, as in any class.

CAN YOU EARN CREDIT OFF-CAMPUS — AND HOW MUCH?

If working independently and managing your own studies suits your learning style, you may want to complete a sizable chunk of college credits in this way. Some schools allow this to a greater or lesser extent; others not at all.

At one extreme we find programs in which *all* credit is earned off-campus by independent study. There may not even be a campus; sometimes all you have are an administrative staff and a vast computerized file to keep track of student progress. Such programs, known as *external degree programs,* include the New York State Regents External Degree Program, New Jersey's Thomas A. Edison College, and Connecticut's Board for State Academic Awards. Although sponsored by individual states, these programs are open to adults anywhere in America, and indeed, anywhere in the world. You accumulate credits by means of CLEP and similar examinations, as well as courses offered by industry, the military, or other colleges. The work may be undertaken either before or after you enroll. In fields such as music or painting, you can earn credit by submitting tapes or photographs of your work; for students with other individual skills, special evaluations can be arranged. The New York State Regents program, for example, offers B.S. degrees in business administration and nursing, although in the case of nursing, supervised clinical practice must be arranged.

Modifications of external degrees, sometimes called off-campus programs, are springing up all over the country. Again, the bulk of your work is done independently, but you are usually expected to confer with an adviser once or twice a month. The best known of these programs is the University Without Walls, operated by the Union for Experimenting Colleges and Universities in Ohio. It maintains branches on thirty-one campuses in twenty states; you work through the branch nearest you. (The name University Without Walls has been borrowed by many other colleges to describe local programs with a large component of independent study.) In the Midwest you can sign up with the University of Mid-America (UMA), which works through state universities in Iowa, Kansas, Missouri, and Nebraska. UMA is particularly strong in television courses. California provides its own off-campus degree program to state residents; New York offers the Empire State College (not limited to residents, but you have to report at least once a month).

Cooperative education, introduced at the University of Cincinnati in 1906 and now available at over a thousand campuses, is another variation of independent study. Here classes are alternated with productive related work outside the college. For example, a student completing an A.A. degree as an educational assistant spent a semester as a paraprofessional in her local grade school; her responsibilities included the preparation of a detailed written report. Cooperative education students usually receive the standard wage for the type of work they are doing; Northeastern University in Boston reports that this averages between $3,000 and $6,000 a year. They may simultaneously receive college credit. But most important of all is the opportunity to get a toehold in the field. At Northeastern, 25 percent of the students who worked for a company as long as six months returned as full-time employees after graduation.

And remember—even at more traditional colleges, you can earn up to thirty credits for study done on your own. This may consist of credit by examination, cooperative education, individual projects, correspondence courses, or any combination.

Further information on off-campus programs appears in chapter 8.

WHERE DO YOU WANT TO STUDY?

Traditionally, this question refers to the location of the college and whether you are free to move there. Today it has another meaning. What with responsibilities to family and job, many returning students can barely manage a trip across town, much less across country. To attract these students colleges are offering courses in libraries, churches, high schools, community centers, factories, union halls, bowling alleys, and a dozen other places. Courses are provided on commuter trains, tour buses, and cruise ships. Sometimes the course is restricted to a particular group, as when a corporation brings in local college faculty to teach mathematics or business to its employees. More often, however, students are drawn from the entire region, without any restrictions.

Occasionally the setting of a course is noteworthy in and of itself. An architecture class may meet anywhere in town and spend the hour strolling around, looking at buildings. Music and drama courses are often held in theaters or concert halls; art classes may meet in galleries.

WHEN DO YOU WANT TO STUDY?

This question has two parts. The first concerns the specific hours you are free during the day or week. The second refers to the weeks or months of the year you will be able to attend classes. To keep this straight, we'll talk about the college's *timetable*—which, like a railroad timetable, divides the *day* into minutes and hours—as contrasted with its *calendar*, which divides the *year* into weeks and months.

For example, Jerry has a nine-to-five job as an assistant bank manager; his next promotion depends on additional study. He is eager to enroll in a college near his job—provided the courses he needs meet after work. Jerry has no difficulties with the college's calendar, but its timetable may pose problems.

On the other hand, after nine years of teaching grade school while raising her own two children, Anne has had it with the classroom; she is working toward a master's degree in guidance. But with the children and her job, she just doesn't have the energy to study during the academic year. Fortunately the courses she needs are all offered during the summer. When the children start day camp, Anne starts school; she has earned as many as ten credits in eight weeks. What makes her schedule possible is the university's *calendar*.

The usual timetable of college classes overlaps the normal working day: say, from eight to six. This may meet your needs even if you have a full-time job. If you can find a convenient course or two during lunch hour or before work, you have no problem. Moreover, many colleges accommodate adult students by stretching their timetables a little. Thus, a popular computer course may be offered from 7:00 to 8:00 A.M., allowing you to have breakfast afterward and still get to work in plenty of time. Special sections of a course may meet at noon (bring along a sandwich!) or immediately after work. And if, like thousands of nurses, restaurant employees, and others, you happen to work the second or third shift, then conventional daytime classes are exactly what you need.

Otherwise, the usual solution is evening courses, which may run from 5:00 to as late as 11:00 P.M. or midnight. Two-year colleges, which pride themselves on community service, provide a particularly wide range of evening classes. At some colleges, every course offered in the daytime must also be available at night, although not necessarily during the same semester.

The college *calendar* provides other ingenious options. The traditional two-semester system, which left summers free to work on the farm, has given way to trimesters and quarters. Under these schedules students may take time off during the year, or they may hasten their graduation by attending classes year-round. In addition, hundreds of campuses offer six- to eight-week summer programs. When evening courses are offered, they usually follow the same calendar as day classes.

Useful as these options may be, they will not help if you are raising a family or holding a full-time job. But you have other alternatives. Some colleges provide weekend classes, meeting only on Saturdays or Sundays. Concentrated summer courses, two to four weeks long, are available for adults who are willing to spend their vacations studying; these programs often include housing and recreational facilities for the rest of the family. Some campuses also schedule a one-month January session between their two regular semesters. Programs like these can be found at colleges like Harvard and Cornell, which do not encourage part-time study the rest of the year. Their goal, apart from the wish to be helpful, is to utilize dormitories at a time when regular students are off campus.

This does not mean that every college offers every course on an innovative schedule. It does mean that if you keep an open mind about the courses you are willing to take, you may be able to earn some college credit during brief free periods in your own calendar.

WHAT ABOUT REQUIRED COURSES?

Colleges often spell out a common core of learning required for graduation. This core, known as the *required course structure, prescription,* or *distribution requirement,* must be completed by every student in order to graduate. In part the requirement reflects cultural values; no matter what your major, you are expected to recognize names like Plato, Hamlet, and Charlemagne. It may also include a laboratory science or two, a semester of mathematics, or the ability to swim twice the width of the pool. One well-known women's college required every student to pass Physical Education 18.01, which invariably included a tap dance called the Tom Thumb. For years, alumnae reunions were enlivened by masses of middle-aged women lining up to do the Tom Thumb.

Historically, required courses have come in cycles. During the early 1900s there was a trend to abolish all requirements; after World War I they were reinstated. In the late 1960s student pressure again caused the elimination of requirements, and again they are being restored.

Today, the typical college requires at least a handful of courses, including basic expository writing, introductory mathematics, and physical education. Beyond this, you may be offered a choice: for example, art *or* music, history *or* sociology, and so on. Thus, one college requires each student to complete a program of general education, designed to "introduce the student to the range of human learning, modes of understanding, means of judging assertions, and avenues for expressing insight, imagination, and conviction." To achieve this goal, students are required to take one course from each of the first five areas listed below, and two from the sixth.

Area 1: Mathematics, physical science, and biological science
Area 2: Behavioral science and social science
Area 3: Language and literature
Area 4: The practice, theory, and history of the arts
Area 5: Philosophical and religious studies
Area 6: Studies in the contemporary world and its past

Lists of courses satisfying the six areas are published annually, and students are expected to complete the requirements by the end of the sophomore year.

At a second school the student must complete eight required courses; four must be chosen from one of the three areas listed below, and two each from the others.

Area 1: Classical Studies, Comparative Literature, Dance, English, Fine Arts, Modern Languages, Music, Philosophy, Religion, Theater, and Speech
Area 2: Anthropology, Economics, Government, History, Psychology, Sociology
Area 3: Biology, Chemistry, Geology, Mathematics, Physics

This college also has proficiency requirements in writing and foreign languages, and an across-the-board physical education requirement.

Some colleges, including several Ivy League schools, have virtually no required courses. As a freshman, you can sign up for beginning Sanskrit, Marxism in Central America, invertebrate zoology, pre–Elizabethan drama, and symbolic logic. How you cope with them is your problem. At the other extreme, St. John's College, with campuses in Maryland and New Mexico, spells out its entire curriculum, with virtually no modification from student to student or from year to year.

WHAT SPECIAL SERVICES ARE PROVIDED?

A college's special services may include anything from an Olympic pool to dances for senior citizens. Depending on your circumstances, these may simply add to the pleasure of going to college, or they may make the difference between attending and staying home.

Child-care centers. Originally, women were not admitted to

college at all. Then room was made for them—provided they were
academic types, with marriage and family in the remote future.
Later it was conceded that mothers could attend college on a limited schedule, after their children were old enough to go to school.

Today the patter of little feet is heard in hundreds of college
child-care centers all over the country. The great advantage of
these facilities is that they are designed around the specific needs of
students. Usually the center opens with the first class of the day,
and remains open until early evening. Some are cooperatives: you
must contribute several hours a week of your own time. (This not
only helps staff the center but ensures that parents maintain an active involvement.) Others allow you to contribute time, money, or
a combination of both; a few are staffed entirely by outside salaried
personnel. Some centers won't take children younger than two or
three; others can deal with infants. The college may also operate a
grade school, so that your children can remain nearby even after
they have passed the kindergarten stage.

One word of caution about campus child-care centers. Make
sure there is room for your youngster. Otherwise you may end up
just one more name on a waiting list.

Services for the physically handicapped. Today, many campuses provide these services, not only because of ordinary human
concerns but in order to satisfy recent federal legislation. As a result, colleges are introducing ramps, elevators, widened doorways
and corridors, appropriate dormitory facilities, and transportation
from home to classroom—and sometimes aides, tutors, and priority
registration for the handicapped.

Counseling and guidance. Apart from the usual student concerns, returning adults face their own problems. How realistic are
their goals? Are their children being shortchanged? After being
away from school for ten years, what are their chances of passing a
demanding math or Latin class? Do they really have to attend gym
and climb ropes—at the age of thirty-five? What can a mother do
when her three children get the chicken pox, one at a time, and she
misses a month of school?

Colleges have always provided academic advising. Today this
has been extended to include career, health, financial, legal, and
personal guidance. Not only is help available, but it is usually sympathetic, prompt, and geared to the special circumstances of
adults.

Libraries and special equipment. If you are a beginning student, most college facilities can easily meet your needs. However, if your interests call for something out of the ordinary, you would do well to investigate ahead of time. If you are studying an offbeat language or some obscure historical period, where are the books you'll need? Is there a record collection for students interested in music? How good are the video production facilities, theaters, gymnasiums, labs? How many computer terminals are available, and can they be borrowed overnight? Because colleges vary in their strengths and weaknesses, you'll want to choose one whose facilities meet your special requirements.

Tutoring. Private tutoring has always been available—at a price. Today, many colleges view tutoring as their responsibility. Writing labs and tutoring centers, often equipped with impressive audiovisual and computer resources for self-help, may be open all day and into the evening. Not only is there no charge, but equally important, there is no stigma; no matter how good you are, there is always room for improvement.

Amenities. The athletic, cultural, social, and other facilities can go a long way toward making college more pleasant. Tennis courts or a boathouse, a quiet room stocked with records, even a better-than-average cafeteria can help offset those long hours in the library or classroom. Don't let such features govern your choice of college, but don't dismiss them, either. In times of stress, they may be exactly what is needed to tide you over.

WHAT WILL IT COST?

This question has two parts: what are the actual costs of college attendance, and what can you get in financial aid?

College costs, excluding room and board, vary from a few hundred dollars a year to $8,000 or more. State-sponsored external degree programs may be the biggest bargain in the country. With careful planning you can earn a bachelor's degree—representing four years of full-time work—for a little more than $1,000. Public community colleges usually come next, especially for in-state residents. At the other end of the scale are the elaborate private universities, with their extensive resources and research facilities.

Colleges also vary with respect to the basis for determining tuition, particularly for part-timers. Some charge by the credit, but others have a flat fee per semester regardless of course load. Figure it out in terms of your own program. If you are carrying ten credits, a single fee of $400 may be a bargain, but if all you can manage is six, it makes more sense to pay $50 a credit.

However, in discussing the cost of college, tuition is only half the picture. The other half is financial aid.

Financial aid is complicated. It varies from state to state, college to college, and even from year to year. There are loans, grants, special programs for minorities, displaced homemakers, and the economically disadvantaged. If you are employed, your company or union may contribute; if you have been in the armed forces, you may be eligible for veterans' benefits. We'll have more to say about financial aid in chapter 9.

Don't jump to the conclusion that from the viewpoint of cost, the college with the lowest tuition is the best choice. Financial aid is often based on "need"—as determined by the *gap* between your actual expenses and what you can afford to pay. Suppose, for example, you have $2,000 to apply to a year of college. You choose a school where total costs (including transportation, room, board, books, and so on) come to $5,000. The extent of your need is the difference between the two amounts: $5,000 − $2,000, or $3,000. That is the amount you ask for in grants, loans, or part-time work. You may not get it all, but you may get more than you think. If, on the other hand, you choose a school where costs are $2,500, your need is only $500—and you still may not get it all.

Many private colleges have substantial endowments to cover scholarships and grants. Thus, a description of one prominent university notes, "765 accepted freshmen applicants who applied for aid were judged to have need; 765 of these were offered the full amount needed." (The difficulty here was getting in; only 36 percent of all applicants were accepted.) If your tuition is covered by veterans' benefits or a company-sponsored assistance plan, they may as readily pay a moderately higher amount as the minimum. And depending on your own future plans, the clout of a degree from an outstanding college may be worth the added cost.

CAN YOU GET IN?

From the above you may conclude that all signals point in the same direction: apply to Yale. Go ahead, by all means, but please apply to a few other places as well. Yale accepts fewer than 25 percent of all applicants.

It is well known that colleges vary in their admissions policies. Just as you have your priorities, they have theirs; what tips the scale at one college may make no difference at another. However, most colleges take into account your high school average, grades on standardized tests like the Scholastic Aptitude Test (SAT) or College Boards, letters of recommendation, the essay you write as part of your application, and your extracurricular activities. The *College Handbook*, which provides information on all the colleges in the United States and Canada, summarizes Yale's selection criteria as follows:

> First criterion is evidence of ability to do successful academic work at Yale. Diversity of interests, background, and special talents are also sought. Successful candidates usually have SAT scores in the 500–800 range, and present a high degree of accomplishment in non-academic areas.

If you are a transfer student, your college record will be the top consideration, although a high school transcript may also be required. Here, too, admission requirements vary, particularly with reference to the minimum grade-point average and the number of transfer credits allowed. A typical statement of policy, taken from the *College Blue Book,* is that of Ohio Wesleyan University, in Delaware, Ohio.

> High school and college transcripts required. Minimum 2.0 grade-point average required. Credit usually given for grades of 2.0 and higher in equivalent courses at approved institutions. Maximum of 60 semester hours of transfer credit allowed toward bachelor's degree.

Bucknell University, in Lewisburg, Pennsylvania, specifies a minimum 2.5 grade-point average, but requires only thirty-two hours of residency. On the other hand, Harvard, which has even higher standards for transfer students than for incoming freshmen, couches its requirements in carefully neutral terms.

High school and college transcripts required. No minimum grade-point average required. Each student's record evaluated individually to determine number of transferable credits. SAT required of all applicants. Transfer applicants with more than 2 full academic years of college not admitted.

Requirements may be lower at public colleges, particularly for in-state residents. Many of these colleges have adopted an open-admissions policy; anyone with a high school diploma or the equivalent is assured of admission. A four-year public college may routinely admit you as a junior if you hold an associate's degree from a community college in the same system. This can be a powerful argument for getting an associate's degree if you are anywhere near it.

Finally, there are the external degree programs. Often the only academic requirement for admission to these programs is a high school diploma or the equivalent. Some, including state or municipal programs in Indiana, Iowa, New Jersey, New York, Minnesota, and Utah, don't require even that much; if you seem qualified for college-level work you are admitted regardless of your academic background. Additional information can be found in the *Chronicle Guide to External and Continuing Education,* described further in chapter 8.

Nontraditional programs will be mentioned again and again in this book. As you read, think, not "nontraditional program," but rather, "nontraditional *features.*" How important are these features to you?

This in turn depends on your goals. That's what we'll look at next.

Four

The Reasons Behind the Degree

As a child, you went to school because it was the law of the land. Now that you're an adult, school involves a conscious decision, followed by a substantial investment of time, money, and commitment. What return do you expect on your investment? What is your purpose in going back?

Perhaps you want to advance in your job. You want more stimulation, variety, challenge, authority, money, or all of the above.

Perhaps, for the same reasons, you want to change jobs.

Perhaps you want an entirely new career. If so, you're in good company; it has been estimated that today's young adults will change careers seven or eight times during their lives. Many find their first job almost by accident, gradually advance, and before they know it, they feel locked into a field they never really wanted to be in. At such times it makes sense to look for something else.

Or perhaps you like your job well enough, but it has become so specialized or technical that additional training is essential, simply to stay where you are.

Perhaps you need this degree so you can go on for another one at a graduate school or senior college.

Perhaps you're tired of being compared to all your brilliant cousins who graduated from college. You're as smart as they are, and you can do it, too.

Perhaps you always promised yourself that you would go back for the degree and there's no reason to put it off any longer.

Perhaps you would like to have some interesting people to talk to and some interesting things to talk about.

Perhaps you just love to learn. You want to know something about everything, or everything about some one thing of particular importance to you.

We all recognize that many people who never completed college are mature, informed, prosperous, and altogether delightful men and women. By the same token, many college graduates fall short on some or all counts. The fact remains—personnel managers looking for employees, adults looking for companions, and individuals looking for self-esteem all value a college degree.

In the last analysis, the most telling evidence for the importance of a degree may be the amount of lying that takes place. A private firm devoted to investigating educational claims reports that one person out of three falsified the record to a greater or lesser extent!

COLLEGE AND CAREERS

Undoubtedly the foremost reason for pursuing a degree can be summed up in one word: *careers*. Gary, who works in the admitting office of a major hospital, has been watching younger, less experienced people move past him into choice jobs because they have the college degree that he lacks. Claudine loves working in her children's day-care center, but without a degree in early childhood education, the best she can hope for is a minimal job as an aide. Stanley's private dream is to break out of the nine-to-five office routine and study horticulture. The Department of Labor publication *Occupational Outlook for College Graduates* lists over one hundred careers for college graduates. Apart from such obvious fields as engineering and dentistry, they include:

Accountants	Bank officers and managers
Actuaries	Broadcast technicians
Air traffic controllers	Chiropractors
Architects	Claims representatives

Cooperative extension service workers
Credit managers
Dental hygienists
Dietitians
Employment counselors
Engineering technicians
FBI special agents
Flight attendants
Health and regulatory inspectors
Health services administrators
Hotel managers and assistants
Industrial designers
Insurance agents and brokers
Interior designers
Librarians
Manufacturer's representatives
Marketing research workers
Medical laboratory workers
Merchant marine officers
Occupational therapists
Occupational safety and health workers
Pharmacists
Podiatrists
Programmers
Public relations workers
Real estate brokers
Rehabilitation counselors
Securities sales workers
Social workers
Speech pathologists
State police officers
Systems analysts
Technical writers
Underwriters

No wonder that when adults interested in returning to school were asked to identify the *one* subject they would be most likely to study, 43 percent mentioned some career-oriented field, ranging from business skills to law.

The Degree: Who Says You Need It?

When we claim that a college degree is required for the career you have in mind, we are in effect saying the following: Some outside agency has set standards in this field, and you are preparing to meet them. Exactly who sets these standards, and for what purpose? It could be an employer—maybe the one you are working for right now—a state licensing agency, a professional organization, or some combination of the three.

College and the employer. To the people who hire you, the degree signifies that at the very least, you have a good grasp of your field and can handle any reasonable assignment. This is clear from the way they publicize the job: they specify a graduate who majored in accounting, or biology, or communications. At the job interview they will ask some penetrating questions about the courses you took and the substance of what you learned.

They will also want to know about your related training. "All I wanted to study was languages," says one French major. "When my department pressured me into taking geography and economics, I was furious! But in the end, those courses got me the exact job I wanted." A business administration student can rise above the competition by learning something about computers, environmental management, and law. One advantage of a college degree is that when you choose a major your program will be designed to meet requirements for career advancement.

In addition, as a college graduate you are expected to offer a wide variety of interests and skills. You can hold your own in speaking or writing. You learn from the printed page; when you are asked to study a procedures manual over the weekend, you arrive on Monday morning ready to put it into practice. Your mathematics, if not brilliant, allows you to cope with ordinary business situations. You can work with people of differing backgrounds, including your colleagues on the job. More generally, you are believed to possess something of the insight and understanding needed to get along in this complicated world.

Finally, employers value the college degree as a sign of sheer endurance. If nothing else, it proves that you can put up with short-term unpleasantness for the sake of long-term goals. The sociologist Ivar Berg, who interviewed a number of corporation executives on this subject, summarized their position in his book, *Education and Jobs* (1971).

> The college degree was consistently taken as a badge of the holder's stability and was apparently a highly prized characteristic of young recruits. Most of the respondents made it perfectly plain that the content of a college program mattered a good deal less than the fact of successful completion of studies. The poise and self-assurance of college graduates received considerable attention as well.

Elsewhere he notes that educational achievement is often taken as evidence of potential for promotion, implying as it does such traits as "self-discipline, personality—important in many jobs—and adaptability."

Many firms require a bachelor's degree of all management employees, or even of anyone ever likely to be in line for management training. Beginning administrative positions in civil service usually call for a degree; so do training programs in retail stores, banks, and insurance companies. Some firms even expect it of receptionists and administrative secretaries.

In such cases the bottom line is the degree; your field of study is usually secondary. This applies particularly to government hiring. Because civil service tries to be impartial, a job specifying a "bachelor's degree" often means exactly that: any bachelor's degree, in any field, from any accredited institution. This can be a lifesaver for majors in philosophy, literature, art history, and other liberal arts areas. Andy took his degree in anthropology out of sheer love of the subject and spent the next eight months as a messenger, bank teller, and post office clerk. These experiences made him grateful to pass a civil service test and become an administrative trainee.

In small firms the degree requirement may be nothing more than the personal preference of the owners; on occasion they may make an exception. Terry walked in cold and talked her way into an advertising agency job on the strength of her samples, assurance, and sheer personal style. Paul, with nothing more than a high school diploma, was hired as a stock clerk, but he was so energetic and resourceful that after eighteen months he was promoted to assistant manager.

But in larger companies the degree requirement is hard to shake. Ginny, with only three semesters of college, took a job as a clerk-typist. She easily mastered the firm's word-processing equipment, was promoted to supervisor (of herself and the three other word-processors), and was finally earmarked for management training. At this point her supervisor had a talk with Ginny. Eager as they were to promote her, they were held back by her lack of a degree. No, they couldn't make an exception, but yes, they would cooperate in every way. They agreed that a degree from a local college would be as acceptable as one from the state university seventy miles away. They not only provided the tuition aid available to all employees but let her attend some classes on company time. Finally, they made the ultimate concession; she was allowed to enter the management training program two months before graduation.

Professional and state licensing. So far, we have been talking chiefly about employers' interest in the bachelor's degree. In many fields, however, professional organizations or state agencies set standards that include a degree.

This is entirely separate from the regional accrediting of the entire college discussed in chapter 2. Professional and state groups concentrate not on entire schools but on *specific programs* within the school. Thus the National Architecture Accrediting Board examines architecture programs, approving some and rejecting others—regardless of whether the college itself is accredited. The American Physical Therapy Association reviews programs in its field. Each state decides which occupations should be licensed in that state and then sets requirements in the field.

All this reviewing smacks of duplicated effort and conflicting results. Is it really necessary?

The answer is that approval of colleges and college programs takes place on three different levels, for three different purposes.

The regional accrediting agencies want to protect *colleges and universities.* They intend the word *college* to retain a sense of seriousness, stability, and intellectual rigor. So they visit institutions and screen out those that fail to meet the mark.

Professional agencies want to protect the *standards of the profession.* They achieve this by "certifying," or approving, applicants on the basis of courses completed, practical experience, and/or examinations. As part of their responsibilities they pass upon college programs in their area. Their standards are usually high—among the highest prevailing in the field. Thus, the American Dietetic Association lets the world know that graduates of ADA-approved programs have all the expertise and skill anyone could possibly want. The National League for Nursing has recommended that all nurses hold a bachelor's degree by 1985; at present, fewer than half have the degree.

Finally, the *state* wants to protect the *health and welfare of its citizens.* Therefore every state requires licensing or registration in a variety of occupations, including the health professions, teaching, architecture, engineering, law, and accounting. A specific college degree is often one of the requirements; in particular, A.S. and A.A.S. degrees may be important in technological fields.

Sometimes licensing requirements have a loophole; you are required to have a degree "or its equivalent." This is designed to protect experienced workers, who can thus remain in the field without returning to school. Beginners find that it is much easier to proceed through the usual college channels.

Not only do requirements vary from one state to the next, but in some fields both state and professional agencies set requirements—not necessarily the same! It is natural to ask, why don't all these groups get together and arrive at a single set of standards?

In some professions this is exactly what has taken place. In law, for example, virtually all states have turned over the responsibility for certification to the American Bar Association. And sometimes, as in library science, the professional organization is so solidly established that the state does not have to do anything.

Beyond this, the answer is that there are in fact legitimate differences of opinion. Should an elementary school teacher have a master's degree—and considering starting salaries, is it realistic to require one? Must accountants be college graduates, or is it enough that they be skilled in their own area? Does acupuncture require licensing, or is it just a fad? Professional agencies accuse states of being slipshod; states accuse professional agencies of being unnecessarily strict.

To see how complicated the situation can get, consider a single field: accounting. Here the top professional level is that of Certified Public Accountant, required by all states for public practice. This involves passing an examination given by the American Institute of Certified Public Accountants. The same examination is used nationwide; so far, so good. However, the job of deciding who's qualified to take the CPA exam has been left to the individual state boards of accountancy. Some states require CPA candidates to be college graduates; others do not. Most states also require candidates to offer at least two years' experience; a few do not.

To confuse things further, some states license a lower-level category known simply as "public accountant." This has nothing to do with being a CPA. The requirements are spelled out by the state and call for no more than an associate's degree.

Meanwhile, many employees sit at their desks and do the firm's accounting, without meeting any of the above requirements. However, they can hardly call themselves accountants or apply for jobs in the field.

This system of overlapping and even conflicting sets of standards often means that you must exert particular care in choosing your program.

If a state has licensing requirements in your field, the situation is simple. You *must* meet those requirements to practice in that state. Anything else is illegal. Even a cooperative employer could not offer you a job, except possibly as a low-paid assistant to someone who already has the license.

If a professional organization has set standards in your field—even if they are not compulsory—you *should* meet those standards to have a chance at the best jobs.

If your field is one with separate state and professional requirements, you should try to meet both.

Some employers specify only the state license, but in this case you are not likely to command the highest level of responsibility or salary. In 1981 a group of nursing students brought suit against a well-known accredited college, alleging that staff members in the school's new nursing program had promised that it would be accredited by the National League for Nursing. For its part, the college claimed that although accreditation had been expected, no promises were ever made. In any case, the accreditation was not granted. These students can still graduate and work as nurses, but the best-paying jobs with the greatest opportunities for advancement may well be closed to them.

If you are working toward a degree in order to satisfy licensing or certification requirements, begin by finding out what these requirements are. If a state agency is involved, send a letter of inquiry; a state-by-state list of addresses appears in Appendix 1. A very simple letter will do the job: something like this.

Gentlemen,
I am interested in Michigan's licensing requirements in the field of ophthalmic dispensing. Please send me all pertinent information.

That's enough. If you are not sure a license is required, send a letter anyway. If you are interested in the requirements of several states, write to all of them.

If you are entering a field in which a professional agency plays an active accrediting role, you will want to write to that agency also. These fields include:

Allied health
Architecture
Art
Bible college education
Business
Chemistry
Chiropractic
Clinical pastoral education
Construction
Dental auxiliary fields
Dentistry
Dietetics
Engineering
Forestry
Funeral services
Health services administration
Home economics
Industrial technology
Interior design
Journalism
Landscape architecture
Law
Librarianship
Medical assistant

Medical laboratory technician
Medical technology
Medicine
Music
Nursing
Occupational, trade, and technical education
Optometry
Osteopathic medicine
Paramedical fields
Pharmacy
Physical therapy
Podiatry
Psychology
Public health
Rabbinical and Talmudic education
Rehabilitation counseling
Social work
Speech pathology and audiology
Teacher education
Theology
Veterinary medicine

Complete names and addresses of the agencies, arranged by field, appear in Appendix 2. Here's a sample letter.

> Gentlemen,
>   I am interested in your organization's professional requirements in the field of architecture. Please send me all pertinent information, including a list of approved programs.

Occasionally your college advisers may offer information or advice. Listen carefully, but follow up with an inquiry of your own. Now and then their knowledge proves to be outdated or incomplete.

What Kind of Degree Do You Need?

Until now, much of what we have said centers on the bachelor's degree. However, the bachelor's degree is only one of several possibilities. There are the associate's degrees—A.A., A.S., and A.A.S.—the master's, the doctorate, and even some special programs, tailor-made for specific occupations.

Associate's degrees. Apart from providing the first two years of a liberal arts education, associate's degrees are recognized in hundreds of career areas. Here's a sample:

Commerce: accounting, hotel and restaurant management, data processing, lithographic offset technology, escrow financing.

Health Sciences: dental hygiene, medical laboratory technology, radiologic technology, nursing.

Public Service: recreational leadership, educational associate, library assistant, police and fire technology.

Technology: automotive technology, electronic engineering technology, industrial arts education, fire protection technology, machine tool technology.

A sixty-credit career program at a two-year college includes about thirty credits of liberal arts and another thirty of specific job-oriented courses, geared to the needs of the industry. So well do these programs meet their goals that in many fields, state licensing agencies accept the two-year career degree, in and of itself, as evidence that licensing requirements have been met.

One problem with career training—if *problem* is the word—is that in some fields demand is so high that students are lured out of college and into well-paying jobs before graduating. Although the temptation to leave without a degree is understandable, it is probably a poor idea in the long run. For one thing, a particular field can become overcrowded, often when you least expect it. In the 1970s, data processors were at such a premium that even beginners were hired. Now supply is beginning to catch up; over the next few years there may even be a surplus. Then employers—possibly the very ones who initially tempted students to leave school—may begin to demand a degree.

Moreover, to leave before completing your program means that you are cutting corners on your training somewhere along the line. The chances are that eventually you will need that training. Can an A.S. or A.A.S. degree be credited toward completion of a four-year bachelor's program? That depends. The Regents External Degree Program and similar programs in other states usually recognize all college credit, if only as electives. Elsewhere, the school and course of study may make a difference. Harvey found that his A.S. in electronics technology provided fifty-four credits toward a bachelor's degree in electronic engineering. Had he shifted to business administration, he would have received barely half of that.

With an A.A. degree, transferring is no problem; the degree was developed for this purpose. At the same time, this degree is becoming increasingly marketable. As the high school diploma declines in value, employers are specifying the A.A. for a host of office, banking, retailing, and similar jobs, particularly those that involve dealing with the public.

Master's degrees. Historically, the master's degree has been under a cloud; in the nineteenth century the citizens of Cambridge used to say that "all a Harvard man has to do for his master's degree is pay five dollars and stay out of jail." Today it serves not only as a stopping point on the long road to the doctorate but as an important credential in a variety of professions.

One of the most popular master's degrees is the MBA, or Master of Business Administration. This degree is specified by many corporations for higher-echelon jobs, often at dazzling salaries. Whether the demand for an MBA continues will depend on the quality of the programs and the performance of their graduates. Meanwhile, it is so popular that Southern Illinois University has been offering an MBA at off-campus locations as far afield as California.

Less glamorous but far more common are the master's degrees required for licensing in education, psychology, and the social sciences. A master's degree in education is required for high school teaching, educational administration, bilingual instruction, education of the physically handicapped and the emotionally disturbed, the very old or very young, and a host of other specializations. Social workers and psychotherapists are usually required to have a master's; so are counselors in fields like rehabilitation, child welfare, and gerontology.

Apart from the courses required for the degree, licensing agencies may also specify a substantial block of supervised practice, ranging from several hundred hours to a thousand or more. (A thousand hours is ten hours a week for two years!) When all that is finished, the applicant faces a stiff licensing examination.

None of this is easy on students, and it is not meant to be. It is meant to protect the physical and mental health of the clients drawing on their professional services. Recently a number of "psychologically oriented" schools have sprung up, offering allegedly quick-and-easy degrees. Many of these schools are not accredited, and their degrees may not be acceptable for licensing purposes. The American Psychological Association has given its approval to selected programs; employers often insist on a degree from an APA-approved school.

Other fields in which a master's may be specified, for professional advancement if not for licensing, include physical and occupational therapy, dietetics, library science, and public health nursing. If supervised clinical practice is not a requirement, the master's is comparatively easy to obtain. It requires between 30 and 36 credits—a drop in the bucket, compared to the 120 required for a bachelor's degree—and the preparation of a master's thesis may be optional.

Doctor's degrees. Even today, doctorates are demanding and relatively uncommon degrees. Satisfying the requirements often takes up to eight years. The formidable "dissertation," an original research project which may itself take several years, is always part of the program. So is the mastery of one or more foreign languages.

In 1979 American colleges awarded close to a million bachelor's degrees and about 300,000 master's, but fewer than 33,000 doctorates. Of the master's degrees, 40 percent were in education and another 15 percent in business management. At the doctoral level, education continued to be the most popular field, with 24 percent of the total. This was followed by social sciences (11 percent), biological sciences (10 percent), and physical sciences (10 percent). The popularity of a doctorate in science lies in the fact that no researcher can hope to enter the field without it. For the same reason, the proportion of master's degrees in this area is negligible—less than 4 percent of the total.

Many students take a master's degree before going on to the doctorate, but one is not a prerequisite for the other. It has even been claimed that they pull in opposite directions. The master's tends to be specific and career-oriented, while the doctorate emphasizes theory and research. Some employers shy away from

Ph.D.s; they want their staff to have a more practical, nuts-and-bolts approach. However, the doctorate is essential in university teaching, in scientific research, and in certain key positions in government and industry.

College, tailor-made for you. No matter how specialized your interests, today's flexible new programs often enable you to plan a course of study that provides virtually everything you need. Such programs may lead to any degree, from the A.A. to the Ph.D.—or to no degree at all. What they have in common is that they teach you what you need to know.

Amy had completed two years as a computer science major when a cousin suggested she might be interested in traffic management, the science of moving merchandise from source to ultimate destination. The work required a wide range of courses, from linear programming to real estate, from geography to business administration. However, Amy's college was willing to cooperate. What was not offered within the school she handled through independent study. She persuaded a local plastics factory to serve as a case study, and in fact suggested some modifications that saved the shipping department nearly $40,000 a year. Her degree is still in computer science, but her work yields an impressive salary, and she is planning to branch out on her own as a consultant.

David, an assistant in a local community center, had never even considered college until his imagination was fired by the idea of sports therapy with disadvantaged teen-agers. To prepare himself, he would need not only physical education but psychology, political science, sociology—with a little urban studies and law on the side. The typical bachelor's program barely began to meet his needs. Instead, he turned to a contract learning program offered by a branch of the University Without Walls. A core of studies in physical education and social science was completed at a local college. For the rest, he designed independent study projects around his job, working under the senior staff at the community center. His degree was custom-tailored to his needs.

Kay already had an M.A. in education when she thought of introducing number concepts to first-graders through body movement. After filling in a background in physiology and dance, she enrolled as a nonmatriculated student at a nearby university. Here—with the support of two professors, one in mathematics education and the other in kinesthetics—she carried out a series of experiments, and discovered that she was getting through to children who had trouble with more routine approaches. The eighteen credits she accumulated have never been used, although she may apply them toward a doctorate some day. More important, she has described her approach at several meetings and is becoming known as a specialist in the field.

Programs like these begin with *you:* you must know what you want and what it takes to get there. Then you locate an existing program—or, if none exists, design one of your own and persuade some college to let you try it. That is not always easy or even possible. Laboratory sciences can rarely be completed away from campus; computer courses presuppose the necessary equipment. Compromises may be unavoidable: you choose between passing up an organic chemistry course or driving seventy miles to take it. The reward is that you graduate with precisely the preparation needed for the career you have in mind.

Changing Careers

Career change is one of the phenomena of contemporary life. It is almost uniquely American. That adults thirty, forty, even fifty years old can pause, review their lives, and do a professional about-face is a marvel to visitors from abroad. Over the past twenty years, the average college graduate has changed careers three or four times. Over the next twenty, it is predicted that career change will occur seven or eight times in the average working life.

One explanation is the incredible rate of technological change. Another is America's traditional emphasis on individual initiative. You can make your opportunities; you don't have to be locked in.

Often, the career change consists of advancing in one's present field. An educational paraprofessional prepares to become a teacher. An emissions-control mechanic becomes interested in improving the process and learns engineering. Or a bank teller moves up in the hierarchy through loan teller, loan officer, credit analyst, and assistant manager, and then decides to study human relations, which he feels are at the heart of the banking business.

Other changes are more drastic. A clothing worker, laid off again and again because of seasonal lulls, prepares to open a nutritionally sound snack bar; after all, food never goes out of style. A clerk in a music store switches to a B.A. program in communications. A clerical worker, knowing only that he doesn't intend to spend the rest of his life behind a typewriter, returns to college, planning to sample everything until he can make up his mind.

If you are anticipating a change of career, talk over your goals with the college's career guidance office. If necessary, inquire about vocational testing—or look for similar services from your state employment office or an independent career counselor. If you are making a radical change, you may have to start college virtually from scratch. On the other hand, if you are building on your present career you have a head start; check out the possibility of college credit for experience or on-the-job training. And remember that everything noted earlier about professional or state licensing still applies.

Dollars and Degrees

If you are returning to college for career reasons, chances are that the extra income you expect to earn is a powerful incentive. For years it was common wisdom that college paid off; you began to earn more money directly after graduation and continued earning more for the rest of your life. Then economists took a closer look and announced that in terms of what college cost, the graduates were not that far ahead of everyone else. This seems to contradict daily observation. What is actually going on?

The economists arrived at their conclusion in two steps. First they checked the costs, direct and indirect, of getting the degree. Then, interpreting this as an investment, they asked whether the extra earnings provided a reasonable rate of return.

Direct costs, with ball-park figures in parentheses, include tuition ($2,500), room and board ($3,500), and incidentals like books, travel between home and campus, and so on ($1,000). These add up to $7,000 a year, or $28,000 over four years.

But indirect costs loom still larger. The idea here is that if you are going to school instead of working, you are losing the salary you could have earned. Putting this at $10,000 a year—not very high by today's standards—you are out of pocket another $40,000 over the four years needed to get a bachelor's degree. Adding up the direct and indirect costs, you find that college cost you $68,000, which is in fact a respectable sum.

The only problem is that this computation makes sense for teen-agers attending college full-time, but not for adults like you. If you're attending a state or municipal college, tuition is well under $2,500 a year; it's probably closer to $600 or $700. Travel is no more than a local bus ride. But most important, you probably have *not* quit work to go to college; you are doing both at the same time. So those towering "indirect costs" drop from $40,000 to little or nothing. In short, instead of costing $68,000, as claimed, your education may cost less than one-tenth of that amount. So if you read anywhere that the financial rewards for completing college are not what you imagined them to be, put it out of your mind. The computations are based on the budgets of average, traditional, full-time students. You're not average, you're probably not full-time, and you're certainly not a traditional student.

The claim has also been made that with the United States awarding up to a million bachelor's degrees a year, the degree is bound to become commonplace and lose its value. Actually the trend is more likely to be in the opposite direction. As the high school diploma carries less weight and as the pool of college graduates continues to grow, employers will attach more importance, not less, to a college degree.

COLLEGE AND YOUR NEXT DEGREE

Ricky is well on the way to completing a bachelor's degree in social science, but she sees it only as a stepping-stone to law school. Arnold's A.A.S. degree in electromechanical technology will enable him to support himself while continuing toward a B.S. in business management—or even an M.B.A. Jay is interested in library science; the primary purpose of his B.A. in Soviet studies is to provide entry into graduate school.

In the long run, all these students are interested in careers. For the moment, however, their objective is quite different: they are completing one degree simply as a prerequisite for another.

If this is your situation, then you, like your career-minded classmates, are preparing to meet standards set by some outside agency. The difference is that this time the agency is not an employer, government, or professional organization, but a university. You may be moving from an associate's degree to a bachelor's, from a bachelor's to a master's, or from a master's to a doctorate. Or you may be planning to transfer to another institution, even without receiving a degree from the current one. The steps you must take in any of these cases are substantially the same.

If you plan to meet the admissions requirements of some other university, begin by finding out what these requirements are. It is a good idea to do this now, even if you have another year or two before making the change. If you are going to need a foreign language, a year of calculus, or a few elementary psychology courses, you should know about it at once.

Start by identifying a few schools in which you might be interested, and send *two* letters to each of them: one to the admissions office and one to the chairman of the appropriate department. (You can usually find his name in a current catalog.) In each case explain that you are thinking of attending their institution, and ask what they look for in their applicants.

Answers will vary, but almost all of them will have something to say about course of study and grades. Course of study may specify both the total number of credits and the specific courses. As for grades, although they carry little weight in business or industry, they still reign supreme in the academic world. Nothing is more luxurious than applying to graduate school with a straight A average.

However, strong letters of recommendation also make a difference. So does an unusual background, especially for adult applicants; don't hesitate to mention your three months as a construction worker or the articles you contributed to the Sierra Club newsletter. And ultimately, acceptance may depend on your field of study. In areas like elementary education, where there are fewer and fewer applicants, some colleges accept all comers. In law or business administration, they may be cruelly selective.

In lining up prospective colleges and universities, include some that offer nontraditional programs. Colleges that offer such programs are known to be liberal, not only in their admissions requirements, but in granting credit for previous course work. Moreover, they are sensitive to the special needs of returning adults like you. Finally, to the extent that you want a voice in the design of your own program, you will find the nontraditional colleges far more flexible than the more conventional school.

COLLEGE AND YOU

Employers, universities, and professional groups are not the only agencies to demand a college education. For all sorts of personal and psychological reasons, you may demand it of yourself.

For many adults, including some who have attained the highest levels in business, industry, or the performing arts, the completion of college is a virtual obsession. However broad their reading and experience, they want the sense of achievement that comes with earning a degree. Today, the goal is readily attainable. Parents are enrolling with their children; even grandparents are no longer an anomaly in the modern classroom.

In 1979, a fifty-one-year-old woman, wife of a judge and mother of fifteen—that's right—children, received a B.S. degree alongside her daughter. "I feel you enjoy life more," she said, "when you know more of art, science, anything, by learning. It opens up life a little bit more to you." A year later a retired journalist with nine published books made headlines by receiving a bachelor's degree from Harvard. Despite his impressive career, he perceived the degree as a bit of unfinished business waiting to be completed. A study of adults graduating from nontraditional colleges found that the satisfaction of earning the degree was by far their most important goal.

But even more exciting than returning for a degree is returning for the sheer pleasure of learning. If this is your impetus, you have an adventure in store. You will discover that using your brain, like using your muscles, leaves you glowing, happy, and eager for more. An interest in botany may lead you to study the tulipomania of the seventeenth century, when noblemen exchanged fortunes for a handful of bulbs, and this in turn will prompt you to examine the magnificent flower paintings of the time. If you're studying math, you may come upon a seventy-year-old book that covers the exact content of your own modern algebra text, but so much better that you will use it for the rest of the semester. When term papers are due, you may come to class empty-handed, explaining that there was "just one more reference" you wanted to check; later your paper will be returned with the comment, "Worth waiting for." In short, you will become a confirmed school-aholic, and love every minute of it.

You will be in good company. In a survey of adult students, 55 percent claimed that becoming better informed was a "very important" reason for continuing their studies; 32 percent cited as very important the satisfying of their own curiosity.

Norman is an example. Three years out of the navy, he earned a good salary as a dental technician, enjoyed sports, and had enough friends to keep him busy. There was nothing wrong with his life, but there was nothing very right with it either. It was time for a change.

That's when Norman went back to college. Now he wonders why he waited so long. "They're stretching my mind," he explains. "They have me doing some real thinking, for the first time in years!" He has not chosen a major yet, but he is veering toward political science. Government was something he had always taken for granted; now he is discovering the causes and effects.

Norman's words are echoed on all sides. Julia, who originally left college to take an office job, returned last September. "I don't know yet whether I'll finish. I don't even know what I can and can't do. But I'm staying until I find out!" She received a C− on her first paper, but it didn't matter. "That paper has six pages—well, five and a half—of ideas I never knew I had!"

For many adults college promises exactly this kind of breakthrough. Their days go smoothly—perhaps too smoothly—but their work has become routine and their friends a little predictable. They never seem to function at full capacity; like Julia, many can only guess at what their capacity might be.

In college, they come to grips with compelling and often thorny issues. They find that far from having only two sides, an important question may have twenty, or two hundred. They discover new role models in the faculty members who, however abstracted or impersonal, have in fact devoted their lives to serious analysis or research. They become acquainted with classmates of all ages who have chosen to attend college, often at some personal sacrifice. Their academic careers become a series of triumphs, small and large. Even if they do not stay for the degree, they remain attuned to a new excitement and potential in the outside world and to new resources within themselves.

On the face of it, these students, returning to college simply to suit themselves, enjoy a measure of freedom denied to their career-minded colleagues. They can turn their backs on the sticky issues of licensing and accreditation. They can take any courses that capture their imagination, in any college they like.

In practice it's not that simple. Phyllis sold shoes by day; in the evening she studied English literature for the sheer pleasure of learning it. But by the time she graduated, it was apparent that she could not remain in selling much longer. She needed a new kind of work to match the new person she had become. She took a cut in salary to become an assistant editor in a small publishing house, and is considering going for a master's degree in library science.

Like Phyllis, most adults are happiest when their work draws upon their highest capabilities. In college they experience the joy of exercising their minds, of solving problems through their own intellect and creativity. That's when their old jobs waiting tables, typing memos, or driving a cab become unacceptable. Instead, the new graduates make radical career changes, at a beginner's salary if necessary, in return for the privilege of utilizing their newly discovered powers. The degree, originally pursued for purely intellectual reasons, does double duty: it provides entry into a new career.

This suggests that even if the immediate impetus for returning to college is to satisfy your own psychological needs, it still makes sense to choose a recognized program in an accredited school. You never know when you will need it. The case is even stronger if you enjoy college so much that you start looking ahead to graduate school. Admissions officers have little sympathy with dilettantes; they will evaluate your record every bit as stringently as that of the most avid preprofessional.

Now it's time to ask yourself, what are *your* goals in returning to college?

You will undoubtedly have more than one; the average reentry student cites four or five. Apart from the career and personal factors mentioned above, you may include such goals as understanding community problems, studying your culture, furthering spiritual well-being, or becoming a better parent and spouse.

Take time now to draw up a tentative list of your own reasons for going back to school. You will probably modify the list as you go on, but your purpose in returning to college will in large measure determine how you go about it. If all you want is a degree, it makes sense to proceed as rapidly and effortlessly as possible. If you are aiming for medical school, grades will be a paramount consideration. If you want to enter a specific profession, make sure your program has the necessary approvals. College is only half of the re-entry picture. The other half is yourself.

Five

Can I Really Do It?

Returning to college is exciting, stimulating—and scary. Can you really do it? Is it—isn't it—too late? Can you toe the mark academically, with your rusty study skills and long-forgotten grammar and math? How long will it take? How can you do justice simultaneously to your course work, job, children, and spouse? And if you dropped out when you were eighteen or twenty, or bypassed college altogether, why should things be any different the second time around?

The last question is the key to all the rest. Things *will* be different the second time around. Colleges have changed. So have you.

For various reasons, eighteen is a particularly *convenient* age to begin college. It affords millions of largely unemployable adolescents a transition to young adulthood. It facilitates the job of college admissions officers. It is a period when parents are still willing to foot the bill.

But from the viewpoint of persevering, learning, and getting the degree, there is no evidence that eighteen-year-olds deserve a monopoly on the college experience. One third transfer to other schools. Between 35 and 40 percent change majors, many more than once; often the second or third change brings them back to their initial choice. Only a quarter graduate in the traditional four years. And half drop out, less for financial or academic reasons than because they were not sure why they were there in the first place. It's worth noting that of this half, 40 percent "drop in" again when they are older and complete their degrees.

Experts, noting this pattern, have drawn their own conclusions. In 1973 the Carnegie Commission on Higher Education recommended that students be allowed to take a break in order to gain work or travel experience. A study of professionals ten years after graduation found that 62 percent would have preferred to "stop out" for a while before receiving the degree. And a federal report urged that college be transformed "from a 4-year lockstep of 18- to 22-year-olds into a flexible and diverse system . . . in tune with the needs of the young, the not young, the part-time students—in short, anyone who wants to learn." So the fact that you interrupted your studies is nothing new or outrageous; it has been recommended by certain educators for quite a few years.

Does this mean that college is going to be smooth sailing? Not at all. You will be pressured. You will not have time for everything you want to do. You may get furious at the red tape involved in registration, change of program, or financial aid. Now and then, your grades will fall short of what you would like. From time to time you will get bored.

But college always has its problems; that's why the teen-age dropout rate is so high. The difference is that when you're twenty-five, or thirty, or forty, you have new, adult ways of handling your difficulties. Your years out of school have not been wasted. You have worked, you have learned things about yourself, you may have married, had children, or advanced on the job. You're not just older; you're better.

CAN YOU REALLY DO IT?

Of course you can. You are probably better prepared for college now than at any previous point of your life.

You know why you are going back. Studies have shown that neither financial nor academic factors cause some students to persist in college while others withdraw. The one difference between what educators call "persisters" and "withdrawals" appears to be a sense of purpose.

But a sense of purpose is exactly what you, as an adult, are bringing to college. Whatever your reasons, you have been turning them over in your mind for quite a while. You know that college may take a long time, but you also know it's not forever. You know how much it will cost. You are aware of the trade-offs—the chores you will neglect against the pride you will feel on completing some tricky physics experiment no one else could manage; the vacations you will pass up against the dollars-and-cents value of your degree—and you are prepared to live with them. It will take a lot to change your mind.

You have better judgment and you can make better use of it. Your judgment is what enables you to balance half a dozen elusive factors, some of which you can only guess at, and arrive at an appropriate course of action. Do you request an incomplete in your philosophy course and use the next six weeks to prepare an elegant term paper—and if so, will you still be able to carry nine credits next semester? What happens when your spouse, your boss, and your children are all waiting for you to wind up your last semester—and your English teacher suddenly asks whether you would be interested in a graduate fellowship? Or what if you find out, once and for all, that you won't be admitted to the school's prestigious physical therapy program, which was your chief reason for returning to college in the first place? Do you schedule your two-week vacation to coincide with finals week, with your cousin's out-of-town wedding, or with a fantastic Caribbean cruise that will really set you up for next term?

The judgment called for in decisions like these is an earmark of maturity. No one is born with it. It develops over the years from experience, trial and error, a growing awareness of others and oneself. At nineteen, you handled the problem of two finals on the same day by going to the movies. Now you find the courage to ask one professor for a postponement and, when he refuses, to get it from the other. When you were a freshman the first time around, you found yourself floundering in a couple of courses and managed to fail them both. Now you consciously sacrifice one to salvage the other. It's a matter of fitting the pieces into place, compromising if you have to, and emerging with the knowledge that you proceeded as well as you possibly could. It takes judgment. You have a lot more of it than you did ten years ago.

You're going to enjoy it. What amazes adults returning to college is that they no longer cut classes. Even when the lecture drags a little, the professor always seems to say something worth thinking about. Are you and your friends worried about the universe? Aristotle and Galileo worried about it too. Are you concerned about parent-child conflicts? Your anthropology instructor assures you they're as old as the human race. Plato turns out to be readable; Dickens is fun.

Thousands of adults report the same experience. In planning their degrees, they expect their course work to be a necessary evil. Instead they are fascinated. Arriving with a richer background, they find that all their subjects fit into place. Even when the hour drags or the text is hard to read, their learning takes on a life of its own. No wonder that when educator Allen Tough examined adults' reasons for learning, such points as "enjoyment from receiving the content," "feeling of learning successfully," and "pleasure from the activity of learning" were close to the top.

You are not afraid to ask for what you need. We'll discuss this again; it bears repeating. It's not that you think you're privileged. But as an adult, you have learned the cardinal rule of enlightened self-interest: if you have a fair claim to some special course of action on the part of administration or faculty—ask for it. You may get it or you may not. If you don't ask, you certainly will not.

Frances had counted on returning to college full-time once her youngest child was in school. But with the campus ninety miles away, she refused to enroll unless she could be promised a two-day-a-week schedule. The admissions office said they could not guarantee anything. The dean of student affairs claimed there was no precedent. Frances sent off a two-page telegram to the president, discussing the responsibilities of parenthood and demonstrating that, for the first year at least, her plan was feasible. Permission was granted.

Paul had to check the indices of dozens of books when gathering data on some obscure World War I legislators. When a clerk required him to fill out a separate call slip for each book, he asked to see the head librarian. The librarian agreed at once to admit him to the stacks, and his research was completed in an evening.

If these students ask for special treatment, it's because they feel they *are* special. So is every student in the school. The difference is that adults, with their clear sense of purpose, have the assurance to speak up. Their cases are not publicized, but they get what they need more often than you would think.

You will prepare a support system. Even with the most careful planning in the world, there will be times when you are pressured or frustrated to the limit. A support system is the safety net that catches you when everything else goes wrong.

Bob's support system was his older brother Jim. They had never been that close, but Jim, himself a college graduate, was determined that Bob should succeed. When Bob's first-choice college wrote that his application was still incomplete, it was Jim who got on the phone to find out what was missing and why. When Bob received a warning in statistics, the two of them sat down with an old review book and made some sense of the subject.

For Sylvia, it was her women's group. With two college graduates and three "drop-ins" among the eleven members, she never lacked for sympathy or advice. Did they think her botany teacher was picking on her? No, he just sounded like a grouch. Could she possibly pass Fortran programming after being out two weeks with the flu? It wouldn't be easy; perhaps she could take an incomplete and make up the work during intersession. What should she do if every section of organic chemistry was closed and she *had* to finish it this term? Take it at the municipal college across town, and transfer the credit; people did it all the time. No problem was too trivial for their attention; Sylvia vows that when her name is called out at graduation, all eleven of them will go up to the platform.

John's support was his lifelong hobby, photography. A month before he was slated to return to college, he reviewed his prospective schedule—eight hours a day on the job, plus three hours of class, plus travel time, homework, and study for exams—and decided it was impossible. That's when he locked himself into his darkroom, measured out his chemicals, and began turning out the enlargements he had promised some friends weeks back. For three hours the painstaking work took his mind off everything else. He emerged convinced that he could study on his lunch hour, read on the trip to school, and that everything would be all right.

Your own support system may be any of these, or it may be a spouse, a classmate, an adviser, a parent, a church group, or even a professional therapist. Just make sure it's in place; at some point you will surely need it.

You will find a program to match your own learning style. One student accumulates twenty-two credits by means of CLEP examinations and plans to achieve her college's limit of thirty. She prefers to work at home, comparing three or four texts, mentally talking back to the authors, and gradually evolving her own point of view.

Another shares this idea of working independently—if ever she gets around to it. But with a weakness for jogging, shopping, and television, she needs the pressure of an instructor looking over her shoulder.

A third takes copious notes in class, recopies them at home, and never looks at them again. The mere process of writing is enough to fix the material in his mind.

Any of these may be your best method. Or perhaps your way is to talk over the new material after class, over a cup of coffee.

Students have always varied in their learning styles, but until a decade or two ago, no one thought of doing anything about it. The standard method of instruction was a combination of lectures, discussions, and group tutorials; undergraduates either fitted the mold or dropped out. Today, there is a program for every temperament. If you would rather not be tied down to a schedule of classes, you can prepare on your own for credit by examination. If this is too solitary, design an independent study project jointly with some other students. If you learn quickly—or, for that matter, if you worry about falling behind—locate some self-paced courses. No matter what your requirements, there is an approach that at least comes close.

WILL YOU BE ABLE TO LEARN?

Starting college in an optimistic frame of mind is certainly a step in the right direction. Once you are there, however, the critical issue is handling your course work. And it has you worried.

You last attended school eight, ten, however many years ago. You have forgotten all the math you ever knew and you have not written anything more demanding than a postcard in ages. Even your reading rarely goes beyond the editorials in the daily papers. How can you hope to change your habits, learn new skills, and keep abreast of the clever young students in your classes? If you've been troubled by thoughts like these, let's get the record straight.

First, worrying about schoolwork is natural. The traditional grading system, with its relentless classification of students on a scale of A to F, invites worry. First-graders are terrified that they'll never learn to read. High school freshmen panic at having separate teachers for every major subject, and are convinced they'll never do well enough to satisfy everyone. Even in today's new "no-fail" programs, where low grades are wiped out by better ones, students blanch at doing poorly on their tests. In short, a little worry is reasonable. It's an appropriate response to problems that may arise.

Second, in light of current educational trends, the fact that you completed high school some years ago may be a decided advantage. Increasingly, high school is being written off as a place to learn. We've all heard about the drop in SAT scores over the last decade. Student writing has been described as a "national crisis." Mathematics has been diluted almost beyond recognition; many high school graduates have never completed so much as a course in elementary algebra. As for study skills, yours may be rusty, but your teen-age classmates may never have acquired any at all. In her book *Improving Student Learning Skills* (1979), educator Martha Maxwell writes:

> The virtual elimination of high school homework during the past decade has widened the gap between skills needed to succeed in high school and those required by colleges, and has created more learning problems for college students.

So don't worry about keeping up with your younger classmates. By the end of the semester, they will be worrying about keeping up with you.

Finally, if you do not trust yourself, then trust your college admissions office. They have been screening applicants for years; by now, they have a good sense of who belongs in the school and who does not. They have examined your record, reviewed your letters of recommendation, and perhaps even interviewed you. In the end you were accepted. If, like thousands of other students, you have some academic problems, your college will help you overcome them.

In general, this help takes one of two forms. "Study skills" courses stress effective learning techniques, whereas "basic skills" bring you up to college level in reading, mathematics, and writing.

Study skills. The content of study skills courses includes such topics as using one's time effectively, identifying important ideas in lectures or books, taking notes, test-taking techniques, and coping with anxiety. Returning adult students may be assigned to special sections, taught by instructors familiar with their problems.

Study skills courses are often required of all entering freshmen and there is certainly some benefit to be derived from them. On the other hand, Maxwell has suggested that for many students the issue is not how *well* they study, but how *much;* some have managed to keep study time to a rock-bottom minimum throughout their academic careers. "They are quite capable of improving," she writes, "once they can be convinced that intensive studying and practice are necessary." The implication is that if you set aside the traditional two hours of outside work for each hour of class, and then let yourself be guided by your own standards, intellectual curiosity, and common sense, the study skills you already possess may prove more than adequate to the task.

Basic skills. Basic skills courses, also described as "remedial," "developmental," or "compensatory," are now offered in virtually every two-year college and in many four-year colleges as well. Prospective students are screened by means of high school records, scores on tests or writing samples, and sometimes field of study. There is considerable variation from college to college. Some schools *mandate* the indicated remediation; others merely recommend it. Some allow credit toward graduation; others do not. The content also varies widely, particularly in mathematics; topics considered remedial at one school receive college credit at another.

Of the three remedial subjects, the most terrifying is mathematics. You were traumatized by flash cards in the third grade, and have not learned anything since. Or you knew it once but forgot everything. "It's like going to the dentist," one student confessed, "I know it has to be done, I know it's good for me, but I keep putting it off."

Cheer up. Math instructors are prepared to deal with the problem. You are not the worst student they have ever encountered; in fact, if you are about average, then half the class is weaker than you are. New teaching techniques have been developed to improve not only your mathematics but also your frame of mind.

"Math anxiety" workshops are springing up everywhere, particularly for adult women. As the women gain assurance, their learning improves; as their learning improves, they gain still more assurance. The program becomes an immensely rewarding upward spiral from which they emerge with new self-confidence in all areas.

If basic skills are your problem, you might want to get started even before returning to college. Special reading courses, designed to improve both speed and comprehension, are a good beginning. Such courses are usually available at adult learning centers or YW/YMCAs; you may even find one at the college you are planning to attend. Math anxiety workshops can also be found in or out of college. Or you may use a tutor to help you brush up on arithmetic and elementary algebra (which is as much math as you are likely to need); if your friends or family cannot do the job, check with the student employment office of your nearest college. As for writing, perhaps the best way to help yourself is to write as much as you can. Keep a diary; send off letters to the local newspapers. Again, you could look for someone to help with the mechanics of writing, but you will be overcoming a much greater obstacle on your own: the challenge of translating ideas into written words.

There is another way of looking at basic skills programs. Apart from course work or degrees, you will need these skills for all sorts of tests, screenings, and job openings you cannot even anticipate today. Those stupid percentage problems turn up on civil service tests. Vocabulary drills may get you past the Graduate Record Exam. If you missed out on this material the first time around, the college's remedial program may be your best, if not your only, chance to catch up.

Nonetheless, students tend to resent the basic skills programs. The label "remedial" is seen as a stigma—despite the fact that half the students at the University of California at Berkeley require writing remediation, and two-thirds of the entering freshmen at the City University of New York require it in math. In any case, students object to spending time and money on courses they don't want, aren't sure they need, and which don't advance them toward a degree.

The experts share their misgivings. Mathematics, essential in some areas, may have little bearing on subjects like literature or studio art. Students with reading difficulties can compensate by developing their listening and note-taking skills, or by choosing courses with videotape or similar resources. And writing may play a secondary role in fields like computer science or chemistry.

So if you are still bothered by the idea of basic skills courses, perhaps you can manage without them. Check it out before settling on a college. Find out which schools mandate remediation and how much, how students are screened, and whether the work carries college credit. Track down the course content: in mathematics, for example, some colleges require only arithmetic, while others consider trigonometry and logarithms "remedial." *We do not recommend that you bypass basic skills,* but if the prospect of having to take remedial courses can keep you from going back at all, it may be worth investigating alternatives.

Finally, if some skills areas really set your teeth on edge, choose your courses accordingly. If you hate library research, steer clear of a major like literature or social science. Granted, you can get through one or two such courses if the college requires them, but don't be masochistic about it—avoid those fields if you can. You will probably do much better in something like health science or geology and enjoy every minute.

HOW LONG WILL IT TAKE?

The answer to this question is another: how much time do you have? How soon do you need or want the degree? How many hours a week can you devote to it?

Whatever your timetable, plan to obtain as much credit as you can for previous learning, including formal and informal classes, life experience, on-the-job courses, and every other source you can think of. We discuss this further in chapter 7.

Beyond that, it's up to you. If you have major family or job responsibilities, a reasonable starting point is to assume that you can proceed at half the traditional full-time rate. The traditional load is about thirty credits a year; begin by aiming for twelve or fifteen. Attending summer school can accelerate the process; no-credit remedial courses will slow it down. Overloading—signing up for more than you can properly handle—and then hoping you will muddle through is probably the worst thing you can do. Not only will it wreck you physically and mentally, but it will delay you in the long run.

At first glance this suggested rate of progress is dismaying. "It'll take me four years," you may protest. "I'll be thirty-three before I'm done!" That's right. On the other hand, you will be thirty-three in four years in any case. This way, you will have a degree to go with it; otherwise, you may still be talking about going back some day.

However, if you are bent on speed, it can be done. Despite the warning about *overloading,* only you can decide what the word means to you. One student with a full-time job finds six credits a manageable load. Another can handle as many as nine; with an extra course or two during summer session, she has cut her total time almost in half. Correspondence courses, contact programs, and other forms of independent study often allow you to work at your own pace, matching or even surpassing the typical full-time progress rate. It helps if you know exactly where you are headed and can subordinate everything else to your studies. Records show that a handful of people have embarked on external degree programs and completed the requirements from scratch in two years, while simultaneously holding down a job! We don't recommend it, but it has been done.

More typical are students like Albert, who is maintaining a steady pace of one CLEP examination every two months. He also scheduled two challenge examinations in European history, a field he had always enjoyed reading about. He took the tests with no additional preparation and passed them both—not gloriously, to be sure, but the B and the C he received earned him six credits and saved several months.

Rhoda took the opposite path. With two children and an occasional free-lance singing assignment, she completed a master's in musicology one course at a time. Even with summer school, it took her four years, but she never felt pressured and she extracted the full flavor of every class. Proceeding slowly also pays off if you attach importance to your grade-point average. Some students compromise by skimming through the required courses and saving their energies for courses in their major field.

Of course, the timetable you set assumes that once you return to school, you will attend regularly. But financial or health problems may force you to change your plans. One student found he could enroll only for the fall semester; he worked in a garden supply shop and things were much too hectic in the springtime. But stopping out in this way is no problem. The work you have completed will be on record when you are ready to resume—even if it's not until your youngest child is in school.

One word of caution. Proceed as quickly or as slowly as you like, but beware of any school that promises a degree in six months. The quality and value of such a degree are suspect, to say the least. Check the school's accreditation with particular care; their degree may not be worth anything at all.

HOW CAN YOU DO JUSTICE SIMULTANEOUSLY TO YOUR COURSE WORK, JOB, CHILDREN, AND SPOUSE?

Earlier in this chapter we noted that one thing in your favor is judgment: you have a better supply than you did ten years ago. You're going to need it.

At 5:00 P.M. on Friday, Gene was faced with the following unequivocal demands upon his time:

He *had* to remain at work because the proposal he was preparing had to be on his supervisor's desk Monday morning.

He *had* to be at the college library at 5:30 P.M. when reserve books were allowed to circulate for the weekend; if he was not on time, the economics sourcebook he needed would be gone.

He *had* to get home because his older son had the sniffles, his wife was irritated at being cooped up in the house, and coming home late would only make things worse.

What he did was:

Take home the draft of the proposal. He could look it over on Saturday, while waiting for the laundry.

Decide to get a used copy of the economics sourcebook at the university bookstore. If he paid $15 and resold it later for $9.00, he would have the use of it all term for only $6.00—not to mention the savings in library fines.

Pick up a quart of chocolate ice cream for the children.

Borrow the receptionist's copy of a three-pound fashion magazine for his wife, who would never buy it for herself.

Gene solved his problems through a combination of judgment, resourcefulness, and genuine concern for family and job. That's what you will do, too.

Think of it this way. With all the responsibilities you are already carrying, you are adding only one more—college. If you feel pressured, start with a single course. Or prepare at home for a CLEP exam; in this way you will not be risking anything if you are prevented from studying. Later, as you settle into the pattern of college, you can extend your program to two courses, or one plus another CLEP exam.

Long before you begin, you will want to talk it over with the people who will be directly affected by your decision. If you are married, you will obviously come to an understanding with your spouse; returning to college will make radical changes in both your lives. Explain to the children as clearly, enthusiastically, and honestly as you can. But if you have already made up your mind, don't ask them if they think it's a good idea; what will you do if they answer no?

How much to say at work is another matter. If you expect to take advantage of your company's tuition refund plan, you will obviously have to discuss your decision with your supervisor or boss. This poses no problem if your course work will result in better preparation for your job. If it means starting a new career somewhere else, you may prefer to say as little as possible. Flaunting your reentry to co-workers can generate resentment and on-the-job politicking you can certainly do without!

But having enlisted every ounce of support available anywhere—don't rush to put it to the test. Your manager, who had enthusiastically agreed that a college diploma would make you twice as valuable to the firm, may nonetheless require you to attend a two-week training program smack in the middle of the fall semester. Your son may think having Mommy back in school is the greatest—until you miss his debut as third Indian from the left in the Thanksgiving play. Your closest friends, the ones you thought you could really count on, may complain that you never have time for any fun. If they are good friends, rearrange your schedule to free a few evenings a month. Otherwise, apologize nicely and go about your business.

Learn to set priorities. This sounds like some lofty idea you learn in business administration, but it's just a euphemism for something less glamorous: learn to compromise. Take the old adage that whatever is worth doing is worth doing well, write it on a piece of paper, and put a match to it. Whatever is worth doing is worth doing—period. Ron needed an extra shelf in the linen closet. He made one in five minutes by propping up a board with four empty cans. Eva had been enjoying gourmet lunches with her co-workers for years. Now she eats lunch at her desk while typing her assignments. Allan decided that repotting the Swedish ivy was less important than making a B in psychology. To Lorraine, psychology and Swedish ivy were both high priorities. That's when she stopped examining her children's fingernails at bedtime. A little dirt didn't turn them into pariahs; if anything, it made them more acceptable to their peer group.

If possible—and it certainly will not always be possible—set aside a little extra money to keep things on an even keel. If your physiology professor has lost track of time talking with you after class and Billy gets home from school at 3:15 P.M., a taxi home is not an extravagance. Gene's Friday afternoon splurge cost him $8.00, allowing for the resale of the economics book. If he did it ten times a year, it would come to $80—a low price for the preservation of family harmony. A dinner of store-bought roast beef and macaroni salad can be an indulgence, unless you have only fifteen minutes to put dinner on the table. Depending on your budget, a baby-sitter or once-a-week housekeeper, an extra book or two, a typist to get your reports in shape can all be considered a legitimate part of the costs of college.

Build in some crisis prevention. If you are using a new baby-sitter or child-care center, start a few weeks in advance, in case anything goes wrong. Get physical checkups for yourself and the rest of the family. Save up some vacation or personal business days; if you don't need them for emergencies, you can use them to relax or study during finals week.

Then get ready for crises anyway. Inevitably, there will be a morning when your seven-year-old awakens bright, lively, and running a fever of 103°. The last time, when it was only 100.4°, you gave him two aspirins, packed two more into his lunch box, and sent him off to school. But 103° is something else; you call the doctor and stay home. (The next day, when you have no classes, he's back to normal. Even the doctor can't determine what was wrong.) When your employer insists that you work overtime, you work overtime; without a job there won't be any college at all, and not much of anything else. For that matter, you may get sick yourself. An axiom of experienced reentry students is "Never cut class if it's avoidable." There will be days when it's unavoidable.

With all your efforts, things sometimes refuse to fall into place. Olga, raising a son on welfare and a very occasional money order from her former husband, felt the only solution was an associate's degree in health science. But her son resented being shunted to a child-care center; she was overwhelmed by a fourteen-credit program including biology and remedial mathematics; and within three months it was time to call a halt. Now that she and her son know what to expect, she hopes to return next fall; meanwhile, she is studying the math she needs with a friend she met on campus.

Reentry works—most of the time. If it doesn't, don't blame yourself. Take a breather, work independently if possible, and try again when things have settled down.

Six

Dropping Back In: A Bird's-Eye View

You've made up your mind. You're dropping back in.

You have decided there is nothing to stop you from becoming a geologist, a teacher, a medical technician, or the vice-president of a bank. You've thought it through, discussed it with your household, and concluded that the advantages outweigh the disadvantages—although there are plenty of each.

Congratulations!

Now it's time to map out a plan.

Educationally, you are at a critical point. Behind you is everything you have ever done that can be turned into college credit: not only the formal credit earned in school, but the potential credit from on-the-job training, military courses, life experience, hobbies, outside interests, and miscellaneous learning from a hundred sources. Coming up next is the screening and evaluation of this background by the colleges to which you apply. Beyond that is the completion of your course work through any of the traditional and nontraditional channels described earlier.

The diagram below tells the whole story. Your "before-credits" feed into the admissions process. Your "after-credits" grow out of it. Your before-credits may be scattered, but they will add up;

even you may be surprised at some of the before-credits you will receive. From here on, your studies will be more focused; you will be targeting your own educational goals. The more you have behind you, the less you have ahead of you. The less you have ahead of you, the sooner you can attain your goals.

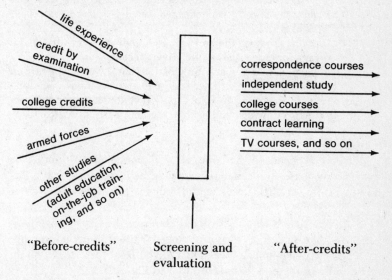

"Before-credits" Screening and "After-credits"
                  evaluation

THE TIME FRAME: MAXIMIZING YOUR BEFORE-CREDITS

If you are like most reentry students, you are probably interested in completing your education—this part of it, anyway—relatively soon. There are dozens of reasons: here are a few suggested by other returning adults.

Whatever benefits you have in mind—career advancement, the pleasure of extending your knowledge, or simply feeling good about yourself—you will start enjoying them that much sooner.

Students often lose momentum somewhere along the line. The closer you are to carrying out your educational plans, the easier it will be to keep going.

Circumstances change. Sickness, added responsibilities at home or work, relocation, all may interrupt your studies. Proceeding briskly will minimize the impact of such problems.

In college, as elsewhere, there is considerable turnover of personnel. If you have a good rapport with certain members of the faculty or staff, you will want to benefit from the association before they retire or move away.

Finishing sooner helps balance the budget. Financial aid is unpredictable, and college costs keep going up.

In many fields, new discoveries make old learning obsolete. Even when the content is unchanged, there is apt to be a shift in emphasis or style.

Opportunities for the best jobs and graduate programs will be greater if your credentials are relatively recent.

Finally, even if you are studying for your own enjoyment, you will enjoy it just as much after you graduate. No one is suggesting that you cut short your learning—only that you complete this particular segment, which will qualify you for a certificate, license, or degree.

You can speed up the completion of your degree in either or both of two ways. You can maximize your before-credits or accelerate your after-credits. Unfortunately, accelerating your after-credits is dangerous.

Maybe that is why it attracted Hannah; she likes to live dangerously. She signed up for four courses while simultaneously juggling a thirty-five-hour-a-week job, a love life of sorts, and a circle of friends. In the end, her record looked like this:

Spanish II	C
Psychology	Inc.
Math I	F
Speech I	D

Result? Six credits, with a D average. If she had registered for only the first two courses, it might have looked like this:

Spanish	A
Psychology	B

The same six credits at half the cost, a tenth the fuss and commotion, and an average between A and B. Your experience may not be as disastrous as Hannah's, but you are taking chances all the same.

The other option—maximizing your before-credits—has several advantages. One is that it makes use of achievements of which you can be proud: your own credit-worthy experiences, or the subjects you learned independently, simply because you cared about them.

Another is that for relatively little additional effort, you can earn a substantial amount of credit. Keep in mind that theoretically, at least, the typical three-credit course requires over one hundred hours of class attendance and study. The same hundred hours devoted to preparing a life experience portfolio may yield between six and fifteen credits—perhaps more at some schools. A mere five hours spent tracking down two advanced placement courses taken in high school can give you six credits. Thirty hours used to brush up for a CLEP exam in a subject you already know can provide another four credits—earned at your own convenience, before you even formally enroll in college.

Finally, maximizing before-credits is risk-free. You may gain a lot or you may gain a little, but you can hardly lose. The worst that can happen is that someone will say no. There is no damage to your transcript, your purse, your academic reputation, or, we hope, your ego.

The next chapter tells how to do it.

Seven

Maximizing Your Before-Credits

You may be closer to a degree than you realize if you have done any of the following:

> Completed some college-level courses.
> Read widely in a field of interest to you.
> Served in the armed forces.
> Received on-the-job training.
> Enjoyed a better-than-average high school education.
> Worked as a volunteer in your community.
> Sharpened your skills in a field that normally requires formal academic training.

How much closer depends on your background, your choice of school, and in part on how you present yourself. It's a matter of identifying anything you have ever done that can be equated with college-level study, finding a college that seems to agree, and unabashedly asking for every credit you feel you deserve.

However, the amount of credit you receive is only part of the story. The other part is—what kind of credit? All before-credits are good, but some are better than others.

Credit toward your major or minor. Suppose you are majoring in psychology. The department requires thirty-six credits, beginning with a three-credit introductory psych course. If you can offer such a course or its equivalent, usually by transfer from another school or by passing a test, then the three credits you receive will count toward the total of thirty-six. This is particularly useful because it allows you to move directly to the next level of your major field.

Credit for required courses (also known as *core, prescription,* or *distribution*). These are the general-education courses that some colleges require for any degree. If your previous work can be applied toward such requirements, you will be able to concentrate more of your efforts on fields that really interest you.

Elective credit. This is the credit you receive for completing any course that attracts you. In effect, there's often a ceiling on such credit, even if it is not explicitly mentioned in the catalog. For example, a college may require 120 credits for a B.A. degree. Of these, 36 must be in your major field, another 12 to 16 in a related minor, and 24 in required courses. This leaves a maximum of 48 elective credits. Anything over that cannot be applied to the degree.

SOURCES OF BEFORE-CREDIT

The most common sources of before-credit are prior courses in or out of college, credit by examination, and credit for "life experience."

Prior Courses

Transfer credit. This is the credit you have accumulated through courses completed at another college; it is recorded on your college transcript.

Colleges are sometimes a little vague about what they will accept for transfer credit. Many decline to publicize any guidelines, noting only that each case is evaluated individually on its merits. Others state that they will usually allow transfer credit for a course completed at an approved institution with a grade of C or better, provided it is equivalent to one of their own. The language of such a statement—in particular the use of fuzzy terms such as *usually, approved* (rather than the unequivocal *accredited*), and *equivalent*—suggests that far from providing hard-and-fast guidelines, the statement may be subject to different interpretations.

What in your own background could be acceptable for transfer credit? To begin, any courses you have completed at another accredited institution. Make sure you include them all. Kevin recalled that three or four jobs back, his company had signed up the entire sales staff for a course in Business English at a local community college. That course, once he tracked it down, earned him three transfer credits. Angela, while still a high school student, had spent a summer studying botany and art history in an advanced-placement college program. She was warned at the time that not every school would accept the work, and in fact her first college turned it down—but her second allowed seven transfer credits.

Beyond that, it depends. One student received credit for an illustration course taken at a reputable but unaccredited school; her portfolio of original drawings showed what she had learned. Another was allowed twelve credits for an intensive program in Portuguese, despite the fact that his new college did not even offer the language. A European refugee presented courses taken abroad; the grading system was different, the course equivalence virtually nonexistent, and the college itself obviously "unaccredited" by American criteria, but she received full credit for her work.

Keep these cases in mind as you review your own record. Remember, the vagueness of colleges in describing their transfer policies may be deliberate; in working with so many individuals, they must allow for some leeway. Even a public statement that a school *will* accept certain courses does not mean it *won't* accept anything else.

But it is up to you to take the initiative. If you believe that you have learned enough from some course to warrant college credit—and if you can document your learning by means of notebooks, outlines, reports, term papers, or projects—then ask for the credit. Go ahead even if the course was taken at a nonaccredited school; even if it was merely a no-credit continuing education course. Your college may very well grant the credit; otherwise, you have lost nothing.

If you feel you are entitled to transfer credit, you will want to get your records in order. Make sure you have complete, updated copies of your own transcripts. If not, order them from the registrars of the colleges from which you are claiming credit. If you are not sure of the fee for the transcript, enclose a check for, say, $5.00; the saving in time and postage will make up for any overpayment. While you're at it, send for your high school transcript, too.

These "unofficial" transcripts will not be accepted by the colleges to which you apply; for *that* purpose they require "official" transcripts, which go directly from school to school without ever passing through your hands. However, the unofficial versions will show you what is on record. When you receive a transcript, make sure all entries are correct; in particular, verify that interim grades of absent or incomplete have been updated. If you dropped a course without penalty, check that it does not show as a failure. Mistakes like these involve lots of time and correspondence, so start early. On the other hand, you may be pleasantly surprised to find that you have completed a course or two you barely remember having taken!

As we have seen, colleges are more likely to grant transfer credit if your old course is equivalent to one they offer themselves. How do you prove equivalence? Usually by producing the catalog description of your course—*at the time you took it.* This is no problem if your courses are recent; the current catalog descriptions will probably serve. But if your work goes back a few years, you may find that course descriptions—not to mention names and numbers!—have undergone major changes.

This means another round of letters. Send one to the registrar, who has files of old catalogs and may be willing to supply the information you need for all courses in all departments.

But in addition, get off a separate letter to each department in which you studied. Include the name, number, and date of every course you completed. Ask, not only for the course descriptions, back when you took them, but also for the author and title of the text and any outlines or syllabi that may still be on hand. It helps to mention the names of your instructors; they may still have materials that the rest of the department has long forgotten. If you are contacting several departments, you can prepare a form letter and use photocopies.

Credit for Noncollegiate Courses. The term *noncollegiate* is self-explanatory: the course is offered by a nonacademic agency such as a corporation, a museum, a cultural center, or a volunteer group. It also includes armed forces courses taken as part of military training—*not* the voluntary college-level courses that military personnel may take on their own time.

As we saw in chapter 3, two organizations—the American Council on Education (ACE) and the University of the State of New York (USNY)—have examined many of these courses and approved them for college credit. Thousands of military and industrial courses have been approved—but so have courses offered by such groups as the YWCA, the Literary Volunteers of America, the American Jewish Committee, and the Chautauqua Institute.

Many adults have completed more noncollegiate courses than they realize. Think hard. Have you ever taken a course preparing you to be a scout leader? A museum guide? A volunteer tutor? A library aide? Did your company provide a thorough, if unofficial, introduction to business law? Have you taken courses through CETA, VISTA, or the Peace Corps? Have you participated in tours that included a lecture series? Marcia forgot entirely about a paleontology course she had taken years back at the municipal science center; she was furious when she learned that a classmate had received three credits for that same course. Gregg seldom mentioned a job he had held with a major corporation long ago—the one he'd lost after a half-year for chronic lateness. But the courses taken on that job could be worth four or five credits today.

If your noncollegiate courses are approved by ACE or USNY, you will be spared the trouble of spelling out the content and value of the course; it has been done for you. But you can request credit for *any* noncollegiate course, approved or not, if you think you deserve it. In this case you must demonstrate the value of the course, through outlines, assignments, papers, or reports.

Again, you will want to get your records in order. For courses taken on the job, write to the personnel office; include your name, employment dates, and everything you recall about the courses themselves. Explain why you need the information; the people at personnel can help you better if they understand the purpose of your request. Military courses are usually listed on the applicant's DD Form 295 (for active-duty personnel) or DD Form 214 (for veterans); course completion certificates also provide proof. For other types of noncollegiate courses, write directly to the sponsor.

Final decisions on noncollegiate courses usually rest with the individual college. Even in the case of an approved course, the college can accept, reject, or modify the recommendation as it sees fit.

Colleges are particularly wary of accepting highly specialized technical courses unrelated to a student's current interests. If you were in the air force, you may have taken a dozen courses in radar maintenance, but unless you are studying electronic engineering, you may receive only a handful of credits for the whole lot. Try it anyway. *Never* decide in advance that this or that course could not be worth credit. Your job is simply to furnish all the information you can; leave the decision making to the college.

Standardized Examinations

Today, several well-known, widely accepted testing programs enable you to earn credit by demonstrating mastery of college-level subjects. These programs include:

AP (Advanced Placement) tests. These are usually offered in high school. If you took any, the scores should appear on your high school transcript. If you are not sure, write to: AP Examinations, College Entrance Examination Board, Box 77, Princeton, NJ 08540.

CLEP examinations. These are administered by the College-Level Examination Program. They are of two types. Five *General Examinations* cover English composition, mathematics, natural sciences, social sciences, and humanities—the areas usually emphasized in required freshman courses. *Subject Examinations* are comparable to final exams in specific college courses, usually on an introductory level. More than fifty subject examinations are available, in such fields as English, foreign languages, history, business, math, social science, and nursing. The tests are offered regularly on more than a thousand campuses as well as at locations overseas; if you live more than 150 miles from a testing center, a special examination can be arranged just for you. The fee is about $25 a test, with a small reduction if you take more than one in the same testing period.

CLEP tests are accepted in over 1,500 American colleges and universities. However, each school sets its own policy on subjects, passing grades, and maximum number of credits allowed. For an overview of college policies, you may want to look at *College Placement and Credit by Examination* (New York: College Entrance Examination Board, 1978). College by college, this book spells out which Advanced Placement and CLEP exams are acceptable and the minimum acceptable scores. It also tells whether you can expect actual course credit or merely exemption from having to take a required course, and whether the procedure is automatic or individualized.

Although somewhat outdated, the book indicates, at the very least, whether a college is liberal or conservative in its policies. Thus, Berry College in Mount Berry, Georgia, granted credit for all five CLEP General Examinations, provided the score was 550 or better. At Salisbury State College in Salisbury, Maryland, the cutoff dropped to 500; at Ohio Northern University in Ada it ranged between 487 and 494. Don't scoff at these small variations; they can loom very large if your own scores run around 490. On the other hand, California State University at Fullerton allowed credit for only one CLEP General Examination—mathematics—although it offered exemption for two others. And Ohio State University in Columbus would not consider the general examinations at all. Similar variations are reported with respect to CLEP subject examinations and AP tests.

For further information on CLEP exams, write to CLEP, The College Board, 888 Seventh Avenue, New York, NY 10106. You may also want to check out the booklet *CLEP General and Subject Examinations* (1979), which you can order for $3.00. For each test it provides a description and a good selection of sample questions.

CPEP, REDE and ACT PEP tests are all related. *CPEP* was introduced by the College Proficiency Examination Program for residents of New York state. It resembles CLEP, except that tests are available in several specialized areas, including criminal justice, education, nursing, and secretarial science. On the other hand, the introductory examinations are limited to history, physiology, and English. *REDE* tests, covering advanced areas of business and nursing, are offered by the New York State Regents External Degree Program in connection with its bachelor's degrees in these two fields. As with CLEP, individual colleges make their own decisions about acceptability and cutoffs on CPEP and REDE tests. If you live in New York, you can learn more about these tests by writing to CPEP (or REDE), New York State Department of Education, 99 Washington Avenue, Albany, NY 12230. Outside New York, the tests go under the name *ACT PEP* and are administered by the American College Testing Program, Box 168, Iowa City, IA 52240.

DANTES tests (Defense Activity for Non-Traditional Education Support) are available only to members of the armed forces and to certain groups of veterans. If you think you qualify, contact the Education Services Officer on your base, the Veterans' Administration, or DANTES, Ellyson Field, Pensacola, FL 32509. Incidentally, DANTES has taken over the old USAFI (United States Armed Forces Institute) program, which was discontinued in 1974; so contact them if you need assistance with courses taken under the earlier program.

Because credit by examination can save you a year or more, it is worth your while to shop around. You may consider preparing for one or two tests right now, even before you apply to colleges. However, subjects acceptable at one college may be turned down at another, so get specific information from the schools you are interested in before you start.

Challenge Examinations

If you feel that you already know the content of a college course, you may, under certain circumstances, "challenge the course"— that is, request a challenge examination to demonstrate your mastery. The test is usually prepared and administered by the individual department. Sometimes, different departments within the same college will have different policies with respect to these examinations; some departments will allow them while others will not.

Strictly speaking, challenge exams do not qualify as "before-credits," since you take them after you enroll. However, you can learn the course content at any time. They are particularly valuable if you have taken courses for which you cannot get transfer credit, perhaps in a no-credit continuing education program or a nonaccredited college. Students have also been known to attend regular on-campus courses unofficially, without registering, paying, or otherwise making their presence known. Later, they collect the credit by means of challenge examinations.

Credit for Life Experience, Also Known as Prior Learning

Life experience credit is not a giveaway. It is a channel for recognizing that many adults, in the course of their lives and careers, have achieved serious, college-equivalent learning that deserves college credit. Most colleges that allow credit for life experience put a ceiling on the total amount. Some have a minimum age; if you are younger than, say, twenty-five, you probably don't have the caliber of experience they have in mind. A number of colleges do not accept it at all. The directories published by CAEL (Council for the Advancement of Experiential Learning) provide information in this area; they are described more fully later in the chapter.

As noted in chapter 3, you do not get life experience credit merely for breathing. Or running a household. Or holding a routine job, no matter how long or how well. We have already quoted the standards at Pace College; those of the City University of New York strike the same note.

> Although all life experience involves some learning, it is not always learning which can be credited toward a college degree. Only that experience which involves a significant contribution to a given area of activity, a theoretical (as opposed to a strictly practical) comprehension of the activity, or which is parallel in some way to the depth and breadth of investigation or original contribution in traditional classroom instruction can be considered for life experience credit. Examples might be contributions to the arts (painting, sculpture, music composition and/or performance, criticism, writing, theatrical performance, stage design, etc.), significant (and possibly creative) activities in politics, political organizations and social welfare programs, extensive teaching, expertise with computer languages, and notable accomplishments in business. These examples, of course, are far from inclusive. Students are *not* likely to receive life experience credits for trades, clerical work, general patient care, homemaking, sales, certain levels of community involvement (PTA, block associations, etc.), and other such activities.

Even when you can offer valid, credit-worthy life experience, the preparation of a portfolio is a major undertaking. A rising television executive examined dozens of college catalogs to find writing, communications, design, and management courses duplicating what she had learned on her own. A businessman presented a portfolio as exciting as a detective story. Would the new line sell? Would he get the financing he needed? Would his renegade salesman steal away his customers? The report, close to 200 pages long, had obviously been prepared with enormous pride, affection, and care. It made marvelous reading.

For all this effort, you have two rewards. One is the solid block of credits you may receive—fifteen, twenty, or more. The other is your own sense of achievement in writing up your life experience for official recognition. The fifteen credits received by the television executive mentioned earlier were the least of it. "My experience was all over the map," she admitted. "It didn't seem to add up. With everything, I could never be sure I'd done anything with my life. Maybe it's a sign of insecurity, needing this outside reassurance, but I'm glad to have it all the same."

One problem with having your life experience evaluated is that from the college's point of view, it is a formidable job; many schools will not even begin until after you enroll. This can have you running around in circles. You want a college that will give you maximum credits, but you can't even determine how many credits you will receive until you choose a college. Later in this chapter we'll suggest ways to deal with this dilemma.

Finally, a warning about duplicate credit. The general principle is that you receive college credit only once in a given area. If your transcript shows a three-credit course in American History, do not request an additional three credits for a CLEP exam on the same material. Colleges are very sensitive about this. To make matters worse, they may not discover the duplication until you are close to graduation, when a special committee will go over your record with a fine-tooth comb. It is depressing to see yourself within two months of a degree, only to learn that a half-dozen credits have been disallowed because of duplication.

Ironically, the same principle does not apply to courses taken in high school. Many a student has completed a high school course in, say, "eleventh-year math," which includes a sizable component of algebra and trigonometry, and then received college credit for overlapping college courses under such names as Trigonometry, College Algebra, or Preparation for Calculus.

At this point, pause to assess your own situation. Identify the types of before-credits that apply to you. Armed forces credit does not much matter if you have never been in the armed forces. Transfer credit may loom large if you left college as an upper junior; if you quit after one semester, it amounts to little or nothing. As you read, pinpoint the information that makes a difference in your case.

STEPS YOU CAN TAKE RIGHT NOW

Before long, you will be caught up in the machinery of applying to college—letters, forms, telephone calls, references, and all the rest. Whatever you can do in advance will help ease the pressure. And there is plenty you can do right now. Today. Tomorrow. Over the weekend.

Get More Information

Using college directories. In order to maximize your before-credits, you need to know which colleges accept each type and to what extent. Several college directories include this information. Thus, *The College Handbook* (New York: The College Board, 1981) tells us that at the University of Kentucky in Lexington,

> Placement, credit, or both will generally be given for grades of 3 or higher on AP Examinations. Placement, credit, or both will generally be given on basis of CLEP Subject Examinations. Maximum of 60 semester hours of credit by examination may be counted toward degree . . .
>
> Each student's record evaluated individually to determine number of transferable credits. No maximum for transfer credit, but 30 hours residency requirement. Maximum of 67 hours of credit transferable from 2-year institutions.

Browsing through such books also demonstrates the variation from one college to the next. At Rutgers University in New Brunswick, New Jersey, "credit is usually given for grades of 2.0 or higher in equivalent courses at approved institutions." At the San Diego branch of the University of California, that minimum grade drops to 1.0; at the Los Angeles branch—part of the same system—it rises to 2.4. Southern Illinois in Carbondale follows the University of Kentucky's policy of evaluating each student's record individually, but "students with associate degrees are granted junior status." And St. John's College in Annapolis, Maryland, which has a unique curriculum based on the reading of great books, allows no transfer credit whatever; "all transfer students enter as beginning freshmen."

The CAEL directories. College directories are a good introduction to college policies on before-credits, but for a more detailed discussion, you will want to check the *Regional Directories of Institutions Awarding Credit for NonCollege Learning* published by CAEL; a sample report appears on page 90. The Procedures for Assessment are particularly valuable. You will discover, for example, that the time required to evaluate your prior learning can vary from a few weeks to more than a year, that the cost ranges from nothing at all to more than $1,000, and that although most colleges require you to be a matriculated student, a few will assess prior learning before you enroll.

There are five directories in all, covering the Northeast, the South, the East Central states, the West Central states, and the West. If your library does not have them, they can be ordered at $10 each; the address is CAEL, Lakefront North, Suite 300, Columbia, MD 21044. (Be sure to tell them which states you are interested in.) CAEL can be helpful in other ways. For some years they have maintained a toll-free number, 800-638-7813 (dependent, however, on year-to-year funding); their regular number is 301-997-3535. Although they cannot provide individual guidance or recommendations, they will gladly answer general questions on prior learning, including sources of additional information.

Contacting Your Colleges. The above references are useful in providing an overview of alternatives throughout the country. They can certainly help you narrow your choices. But once you have identified a few likely schools, you will need to contact the admissions office. If you phone or go in person, prepare your questions in advance, take notes on the answers, and get the name of the person you talk to. If you send a letter, it can be as simple as the following:

Gentlemen,
    I am interested in applying to your college for the _____ semester. Please send me a copy of the college catalog, information on your admissions procedure, and details about the college's policy on
    transfer credit from other institutions
    credit for CLEP examinations
    credit for ACE-approved industry courses.
                      Sincerely yours,

NAME OF COLLEGE

Address

Institutional Description	Public community college awarding associate degrees with an enrollment of approximately 5,900 students. Accredited by the Middle States Association of Colleges and Schools/Commission on Higher Education. CAEL member.
Contact	Director of Nontraditional Studies
Assessment Procedure	The assessment of prior learning is administered by the Life/ Learning Experiential Assessment Program (LEAP) of the Community Education Department. Any person is eligible for assessment after admission to the college. Assessment is based on a port-folio, faculty-made tests or challenge examinations, oral inter-views, and demonstration of competencies.
	Prospective students may attend orientation sessions. Students seeking credit for prior learning work independently, submitting material when completed to the director of nontraditional studies. Students receive an assessment manual, a written description of the college's guidelines and practices for awarding credit for prior learning, and group or individual counseling. Students may enroll in a noncredit workshop that includes preparation for assessment. The workshop costs $14.00 for students from sponsor-ing school districts or $34.00 for other students. The assess-ment fee is based on the number of semester hours the student is seeking for prior learning, at one-fourth the regular tuition rate per semester hour.
Official Record	Credit awarded for prior learning is entered on the person's aca-demic record immediately following assessment and after admission to the college; the individual is not required to enroll in courses. On the individual's transcript, course titles and credits for prior learning are not distinguished from course titles and credits for classroom learning.

For more information, see the state chart.

Opportunities for prior learning credit. (Reprinted by permission of the Council for the Advancement of Experiential Learning—CAEL.)

If you are contacting a large university, indicate which school, college, or division you plan to attend. Even if you are writing to a small college, it helps to let them know what you expect to study. And again, if you are writing to several schools, you need not send an original letter to each of them; nobody's feelings will be hurt if you use good, clean photocopies. Keep a copy for yourself, along with a record of whom you have contacted and when. Three weeks is a reasonable length of time to wait for an answer; after that, send them a reminder.

The Regents Credit Bank

One difficulty with collecting before-credits from a variety of sources is that each new college application must include a copy of every separate transcript or record. This can run into money. Even more serious is the fact that the admissions office may not even consider your application until every document is on file. Tracking down missing materials can sap your energies and destroy your morale.

This problem has been solved through New York's *Regents Credit Bank.* (The credit bank is separate from the Regents External Degree Program mentioned elsewhere; the word *Regents* appears in both because it is the name of the official New York State agency concerned with education.) For a fee of $125, you can have all your before-credits evaluated and, if approved, entered on a single "master" transcript. If you earn additional credits over the next two years, your transcript will be updated accordingly. During that same two-year period, copies of the current transcript will be sent without charge to anyone you designate: institution, agency, business, or individual. After that, you can continue to participate at a cost of $50 a year. The service is available no matter where you live.

Work accepted by the credit bank includes:

College courses taken for degree credit, on campus or by correspondence, at institutions which are regionally accredited or candidates for accreditation.

Standardized proficiency examinations such as CLEP, ACT PEP, or AP tests.

Approved military courses, training, or tests.

Approved noncollegiate courses taken on the job, through volunteer agencies, and so on.

Federal Aviation Administration Airman's certificates.

The credit bank will also recognize credit earned through "special assessment" of your experience or skills not documented in any other way. Thus, you might earn special assessment credit for ability in music or art. Approved life experience credits would also fall into this category.

The credit bank has still other advantages. Every time your transcript is updated, you receive a copy free of charge. If you wish, noncredit work will be listed, although it will be clearly identified as such. Perhaps most valuable of all, only those courses or examinations that you want to appear on your transcript will be recorded and kept on file. What better way to eliminate grades or test scores that show you at less than your best!

From the dollars-and-cents point of view, whether the credit bank justifies its cost depends on the range of your before-credits and the number of official credits you plan to send out. But money does not tell the whole story. You may reach a point when the advantages of dealing with a single, dependable institution—rather than a half-dozen unreliable offices scattered throughout the country—will be worth every penny it costs. If you want more information, write to Regents Credit Bank, The University of the State of New York, Cultural Education Center, Room 5D34, Albany, NY 12230. Incidentally, if you should enroll in the Regents External Degree Program, participation in the Regents Credit Bank is included at no additional charge. In this case, do not apply separately to the credit bank.

Setting Your Priorities

Although it is worthwhile to maximize before-credits, this is only one consideration among many. Issues like field of study, costs, reputation of the college, and availability of evening courses may be equally or more important to you. And for a few students, prior credits don't matter anyway. If you are breaking into a new field, you may need so many introductory courses that a smattering of earlier credits will not make much difference. In the sciences the earlier work may be outdated. And if you are applying to a selective college, you may prefer to omit a transcript altogether rather than weaken the overall impression.

But if you need a degree and need it fast, then review the beginning of this chapter and rack your brains for all possible sources of credit.

Shopping Around for a College

Your records are in order, you have all the information you can get. Now it's time to start looking at colleges. We shall consider this question more generally in chapter 8; right now, we'll approach it only from the point of view of maximizing before-credits.

This takes us back to our earlier dilemma. You want to choose your college to maximize before-credits, but your credits won't even be evaluated until after you choose a college. In short, you are required to act on insufficient information. You gather as much information as you can, evaluate it according to your own criteria, and sail in, hoping for the best.

Maximizing Before-Credit: Some General Guidelines

The following guidelines have been useful to other returning students. See if any of them apply to you.

Nontraditional versus traditional colleges. Nontraditional colleges are usually more liberal than traditional ones in accepting before-credits. For example, the Regents External Degree Program accepts *all* CLEP exams toward its liberal arts degree, provided only that the distribution requirements for the degree have been met. Moreover, there is no time limit; credit earned a decade ago is as good as credit earned today.

Residency requirements. Most traditional colleges require at least a year's residency (thirty credits) for the bachelor's degree. If you already have more than ninety before-credits, this can be an obstacle. One solution is to look for a college without such a requirement; another is to choose an external degree program.

Selecting a major. Selecting the same major as you did the first time around may salvage some transfer credits, as more of your earlier courses will be applicable.

Returning to your previous college. This is a sensitive subject, with arguments both pro and con. However, it can be a good idea from the viewpoint of maximizing transfer credit. Since this school awarded the credits in the first place, chances are that it will accept them the second time around.

Earning an associate's degree. At many four-year colleges, an A.A. or A.S. (although not necessarily an A.A.S.) will automatically entitle you to sixty credits and admission as a junior. Add to this the fact that two-year colleges are typically more lenient in accepting before-credits. So if you have some credits you are not quite sure of, consider earning an associate's degree and then finding a senior college that will accept the full two years' work.

Look for a college where you'll stand out. Colleges welcome students who are a notch or two above average. By concentrating on schools where you are somewhat above the crowd, you may benefit from all sorts of extra concessions.

Preparing for CLEP Exams

Once you have narrowed down your possible colleges to a half-dozen or so, you can save time and money, earn credit, and get back into the habit of studying, just by preparing for a couple of CLEP examinations.

The first step is to ask the colleges you are considering which tests they allow. Identify one or two that interest you, that are widely acceptable, and that do not duplicate material for which you are already claiming credit. Then get to work.

The booklet *CLEP General and Subject Examinations* lists all CLEP exams, along with information on their content; similar materials are available from ACT PEP. You can get them by writing to the addresses given in chapter 3. In choosing a subject, consider one in which you have good high school preparation. While the college exams normally go beyond what you learned back then, a solid high school course in, say, American history, trigonometry, or composition may go a long way toward qualifying you for the corresponding CLEP or ACT PEP test.

Line up some good texts and/or review books. Testing agen-

cies do not recommend texts themselves, but you can get suggestions from a high school or college instructor, a college bookstore,
or a student who has already studied the material. Don't overlook
the public library. In many states, libraries have joined together to
provide a Learner's Advisory Service geared to the needs of adults
studying on their own. These agencies know about CLEP and can
provide the resources you need. Even if your library is not part of
such a service, the librarian can do a lot to help you.

Find a "buddy"—another student preparing for the same test.
The opportunity to compare notes, iron out difficulties, or merely
let off steam will not only improve your grades, it will keep you
going when the sheer monotony of studying on your own threatens
to get the better of you.

If necessary, work with a tutor. College students are often
available; or look for a high school teacher (they cost more), a co-
worker, a friend, or a member of your family. Your children will
love needling you about your mistakes, and you may be able to pay
them in ice cream cones!

With reference to the actual test taking, a variety of pointers
and hints are discussed in chapter 10.

Finally, the new "truth in testing" laws are designed to protect your interests. Since they have been in effect, quite a few cases
of incorrect grading have come to light. If you feel that your test
score may be in error, ask the testing agency to check it out.

Working with the College

In maximizing before-credits, general guidelines are useful, but
they are no substitute for dealing directly with the college's admissions office and separate departments. Although the people you
contact are not likely to make specific promises before you enroll,
they may nonetheless carry a lot of weight.

At the outset, let's distinguish between what you can expect
from the college as a *right* and what you must request as a *privilege*.
Commitments in the catalog or other official college sources are a
right. If the catalog states that an associate's degree is worth sixty
credits and you have such a degree, you are entitled to sixty credits.
If it says "up to sixty-five credits," you are entitled to nothing—not
even the sixty you may have taken for granted. If an official an-

nouncement notes that a grade of forty-nine or better in the CLEP statistics exam is worth three credits and your grade is fifty, you can claim three credits. If it's forty-eight, you can *request* three credits—as a privilege, not a right. Even if your best friend received the credit, they still do not owe it to you.

Rights pose no problem. If you deserved those three CLEP credits and did not get them, point out the oversight in a short letter. You might send along a copy of the college release in which the commitment was originally made. Privileges are something else. Here you are asking a favor. However you go about it, your presentation is a sales pitch. You may appeal to reason, generosity, fear, compassion, avarice, or a sense of fair play—whatever does the job.

Let it be said at once that most college personnel are not merely reasonable; they are downright sympathetic. They consider, not merely the letter, but the spirit of their regulations. As we have seen, they even have built-in loopholes to make it easier for you.

So in working with admissions offices, start by doing it their way. Get the right names, phone numbers, extensions, hours. Make sure you have everything you need, from transcripts to paper clips. Make appointments even to phone; busy advisers cannot always drop everything to pick up the receiver. Work with the organization, not against it.

If you want privileges, show why you deserve them. Jay won over an admissions counselor by arguing that although his previous college was, as yet, only a candidate for accreditation, his particular course of study was considered outstanding in the field. Maura received credit for a D in second-semester Latin by pointing out that the next year her grades were B and A. If you were simply too young and immature to handle college the first time around, come right out and say so. You won't be the first one; returning students are producing such strong records that college staffs are happy to meet them halfway.

Today's admissions offices are sensitive to head count. They may have quotas to fill; they want you. If you have narrowed your choice to a handful of colleges and if the amount of before-credit is a factor in your decision, it does not hurt if, in a courteous and tactful way, you let the admissions office know.

Quit when you're ahead. Watch for small signs: a smile, a nod, a hint that "we can work this out." Even if your request cannot be granted on the spot, approval from the right person carries a lot of weight. Clyde was offering nine rather borderline credits in social science. The admissions officer did not have authority to approve them herself, but she agreed to write a note to the department chairman. Clyde never did find out what was in that note, but he received seven of the nine credits.

One theory has it that administrators are most lenient at the end of the day. They're tired; they want to get home and watch the six o'clock news. If they have already been generous to other people, they will feel guilty about treating you differently. If they've been strict, they'll decide that one exception won't hurt. Either way, saying yes is easier than bracing themselves for yet another battle. That's the theory; try it and let us know if it works.

WHAT YOU CAN DO AFTER ENROLLING

Credit for Prior Course Work

Once you have chosen a college, you will be interested, not only in getting credit for prior learning but for getting the *kind* of credit you need: credit toward your major, credit toward college requirements, or elective credit. Usually this means dealing with separate departments.

Here too, practices differ. In some colleges you see the chairman or a designated adviser. In others, any faculty member can evaluate your prior course work—which means that if you are dissatisfied with Professor A's evaluation, you can find an hour when he's tied up in class and try Professor B. Sometimes you merely complete a form, attach a course description, and receive your answer in the mail; then, if you are not satisfied, you go to the chairman or adviser.

Suggestions from the last section apply here, too. Get your materials in order. Note the names, numbers, and schedules of the people you will need to see. If you have a special problem, you will inevitably come face to face with a member of the faculty.

Underneath it all, most faculty members are reasonable, sympathetic, and even encouraging. They genuinely want to help you—although their idea of help may not coincide with yours.

Properly approached, they will see you by special appointment, discuss your goals, and steer you to teachers whose methods they admire, including themselves.

But they have a wide range of responsibilities, including teaching, research, and administration. Even those who have welcomed the role of departmental adviser may not give it priority. They may schedule only two or three office hours a week. Seeing them can be a matter of luck. Some days you walk right in and spend a half-hour; on others there are fifteen students ahead of you.

Faculty members are rather like modern-day benevolent despots. They have a lot of authority, and they will be glad to remind you of it if you get out of hand. But if you treat them with due respect—not to say subservience—you may find them astonishingly cooperative.

College faculty members share the general concern for attracting students, but more particularly, they want students for their own departments. They want majors—not merely to fill seats, but because they enjoy being surrounded by capable, stimulating students who share their interests. If you suggest to the political science adviser that you are undecided between political science and economics, and that the people in economics were ever so nice, he may allow you credit for a course or two he might otherwise have turned down. Occasionally this works the other way around. If you are an absolute dud in, say, chemistry, a department adviser may accept your previous course work out of sheer dread that otherwise you may turn up in one of *his* classes.

Let's see how this works in practice. You are planning to major in sociology, and SOC 100, Statistics for Sociology, is a departmental requirement. The course description sounds very much like MATH 100, which you completed at your former college. Moreover, you sincerely believe you learned enough statistics in that course to see you through the rest of your studies. You call on the departmental adviser with an eye to convincing him that the two courses are equivalent. Along with the original description of MATH 100, you produce your old textbook or class notes—assuming they bear you out. In describing what was actually covered in MATH 100, you emphasize those topics that overlap the sociology course. If the two courses are equated, you have earned three credits in your major.

However, MATH 100 may also satisfy the course's math requirement. You check the catalog to find the closest math course and visit the math adviser. Of course, you won't get credit twice, but if Math 100 is in fact equated with one of the department's own courses, that's another requirement you can cross off the list.

A word of warning: in any department, some courses are *sequential;* they are followed by more advanced courses in the field. Others are *terminal;* either separate one-semester courses or the end of a sequence. Forgetting the content of a terminal course is not likely to hurt you very much, but forgetting a sequential course can lead to disaster. If you completed a general chemistry course years ago with a grade of C−, you can reasonably offer it to satisfy the course's science requirement, but as preparation for Organic Chemistry it can be worse than useless. If you are told by the departmental adviser that your particular course will not prepare you for the rest of the sequence, it's probably the plain truth. You are better off taking the advice and making a fresh start.

Earning Life Experience Credits

After you enroll is also the time to start thinking about life experience credits. Some colleges offer a special course in preparing the necessary portfolio; it offers guidelines on format, emphasis, choice of a faculty committee, and so on. Otherwise, check with the office of academic affairs. Usually a particular staff member is responsible for guiding students through the process.

Start making notes on your own portfolio. Later, when you are persuading faculty members to work with you, it will help to show what you are planning to do. Examine portfolios from previous semesters and talk with their authors if possible.

A good way to gain insight into your college's expectations is to browse through books written for college administrators, like Peter Meyer's *Awarding College Credit for Non-College Learning* (1975). Meyer discusses in detail the essay in which you describe and analyze your "life experience" and reproduces two such essays in their entirety. He also examines methods for deciding how much credit you should receive. That he wrote for professionals makes him doubly valuable; seeing the college's point of view will help you direct your own efforts.

What happens if, with all your plans and preparations, you are not offered the credit you thought you deserved? Try discussing it with the dean of students, the office of academic affairs, or the president of the student self-government association. Contact the college ombudsman, if there is one; his job is to intervene in grievances of every sort. If all this fails—forget it. Get on with the business of earning your degree.

Eight

Choosing Your College

We wish we could suggest a quick, surefire system for choosing a college. There isn't any. It's a matter of examining the possibilities, eliminating, and gradually homing in on schools that are right for you. Stage 1 is an orientation process; you learn about your options. Then you review these options in light of your own priorities, discovering along the way that some colleges become more attractive while others are ruled out. Finally, you face the hard choices: what *must* you have, what do you want, what can you live without? You end up with a handful of colleges that meet your needs and start filling out applications.

STAGE 1: LEARNING ABOUT YOUR OPTIONS

Examining Directories and Handbooks

College directories list all institutions alphabetically or by state, providing essential information on accreditation, admissions policies, fields of study, degrees offered, costs, financial aid, and a host of other factors. Some of the most popular directories include the following:

Barron's Profile of American Colleges. Woodbury, N.Y.: Barron's Educational Series. Separate volumes for two- and four-year colleges. Includes information on faculty background, age distribution of students, and faculties for the handicapped.

Cass, James, and Birnbaum, Max. *Comparative Guide to American Colleges.* New York: Harper & Row. Lists accredited colleges only. General; may be more useful to first-time students than to returning adults.

The College Blue Book. New York: The Macmillan Company. Provides detailed information on the college environment. No separate information on transfer students.

The College Handbook. New York: The College Board. Well-balanced. Detailed information on fields of study; above-average sections on transfer credit.

Hawes, Gene R. *Hawes' Comprehensive Guide to Colleges.* New York: New American Library. Rates colleges as "good, better, or best buy"; also rates academic and social status.

Lovejoy, Clarence E. *Lovejoy's College Guide.* New York: Simon & Schuster. Inexpensive and readily available, but provides fewer details than some other sources.

For nontraditional programs, try the following. Keep in mind that this field changes rapidly. Titles more than a few years old may already be out of date.

American Council on Education. *A Guide to Undergraduate External Degree Programs.* Washington, D.C., 1978. Well-organized; informative.

Bear, John. *The Alternative Guide to College Degrees and Non-Traditional Higher Education.* New York: Grosset & Dunlap, 1980. Informal and lively. Bear has strong opinions and enjoys sharing them with the reader.

Blaze, Wayne, and Nero, John. *College Degrees for Adults.* Boston: Beacon Press, 1979. Well-organized and very informative.

Chronicle Guide to External and Continuing Education. Moravia, N.Y.: Chronicle Guidance Publications, 1978. A wealth of tables, crammed with information on such questions as evening and nonresidential programs, continuing education, and opportunities to earn a degree. This directory will also tell you which external degree programs have open-admissions policies and whether a high school diploma is required.

Munzert, Alfred W. *National Directory of External Degree Programs.* New York: Hawthorn Books, 1976. A pioneer in the field.

Nyquist, Eward B., Arbolino, Jack N., and Hawes, Gene R. *College Learning—Anytime, Anywhere.* New York: Harcourt Brace Jovanovich, 1977. A classic. Concentrates on the external degree programs of New York, New Jersey, and Connecticut, but so readable and upbeat, you'll want to enroll on the spot.

On-Campus/Off-Campus: Degree Programs for Part-time Students. Edison, N.J.: Peterson's Guides, 1978. Particularly strong on state and local programs.

Rader, Frank. *Innovative Graduate Programs.* Saratoga Springs, N.Y.: Empire State College, 1978. A specialized directory, although graduate programs are also covered by some of the other sources.

You will find one or another of these directories in any library. Browse through them. Look for information on size, location, fields of study, extracurricular activities, church or other affiliation, ratio of men to women and of residents to commuters. Notice how widely colleges vary, even within a single state or municipal system. If you cannot leave home, read in detail about schools within commuting distance; even so, you may want to learn about options in other parts of the country. Get an overview of what's available.

Contacting Colleges and Other Agencies

As you thumb through directories, you may find that they raise more questions than they answer. Is the physical therapy program offered at night? What are the child-care facilities? Can you manage without a car? For answers to questions like these, you will want to contact the colleges or other agencies directly.

The admissions office. The college admissions office can answer general questions on housing, costs, financial aid, fields of study, schedules, credit for prior learning, and the like. Fill them in on your own background, problems, and plans; the more they know about you, the more specific information they can provide.

While you are contacting them, ask for a copy of the college catalog. Sometimes these can be exasperatingly difficult to obtain.

The individual departments. No matter how spectacular the college may be, it is your own department that determines the quality of your college experience. You can ask the departmental head about the size and composition of the faculty, the mandated and recommended courses (and how often each is offered), seminars, honors programs, and internships. Find out about alternate tracks within the major; thus, a political science department may offer tracks in prelaw, teaching, and public service. Inquire about permissible minor fields. Let them know what you have already done in the area, and what you hope to do. Again, ask for a catalog; if they have a spare lying around, sending it to you may be easier than answering all your questions.

This can call for a lot of letters, particularly because different versions are needed for the admissions office and the department chairman. Fortunately, if you are writing to a number of colleges, you can prepare good-quality masters and then mail out photo-copies.

Writing to other agencies. You may remember the College Board in connection with CLEP exams. However, its interest in college education does not stop there. Its Office of Adult Learning promotes training, research, and publications in the field. If you have any questions, write to them at 888 Seventh Avenue, New York, NY 10106; if they cannot help, they will surely refer you to someone who can.

Catalyst is a national organization designed to smooth the path for women returning to work. The agency maintains a national network of more than 150 local resource centers, whose services include educational, career, and personal counseling, job placement, workshops, and courses. Some of these centers charge for their services, but others are free. Catalyst itself serves as a clearinghouse for new developments in the field. You can write to them at 14 East 60th Street, New York, NY 10022.

Do not overlook the public colleges and universities in your own state. Academically, many are first-rate; moreover, both costs and admission requirements usually favor residents of the state. For information, contact the appropriate state agency (see Appendix 3) or your state legislator.

One quick warning. When the replies come in, you will be inundated with material. Set up a filing system before you do anything else.

Interpreting your answer. In the deluge of mail you will receive, you will find two types of material: information and advertising copy. Learn to sort them out. The admissions office may send a sheaf of glossy illustrated brochures: the campus in autumn, the Olympic swimming pool, a "typical" chemistry lab, scrubbed down for the occasion. Its case histories will be glowing—but hand-picked. The admissions office is doing a selling job. Recognize it for what it is.

Far more to the point are the solid bulletins and catalogs with narrow margins and small print. They're not as pretty as the brochures, but they are a hundred times more useful. Catalogs have a wealth of information on courses, majors, requirements, financial aid, retention policies, evening and weekend programs, special services—everything you need to know. Although it may be premature to study catalogs in detail, familiarize yourself with their organization and indexes.

Before we leave the subject of letter writing, let's remind ourselves of other letters, already mentioned, that you may want to send out.

> For questions about the *college's* accreditation, contact the regional accrediting agency; a complete list appears in chapter 2.
>
> For information on accrediting *specific programs,* write to the appropriate agency. State licensing offices are listed in Appendix 1; professional agencies, in Appendix 2.
>
> For information on maximizing before-credits, check the sources mentioned in chapter 7.
>
> If costs are a problem, public and private funding agencies are considered in chapter 9.

It comes to a lot of letters, but each of them can be very simple, and the tailor-made information you receive will more than justify the trouble.

Talking to People

Talking to people can give you an altogether different perspective.

If you are planning a specific career, talk to professionals in the field. They may suggest schools you would never have thought of and veto a couple you had in mind.

If your courses tie in with your present job, sound out your co-workers to learn where they studied and whether they received the kind of preparation they ultimately needed. You can even check with the boss—especially if you are prepared to take his advice!

Talk to the college faculty—allowing for the very human tendency to praise oneself and knock the competition. If you want a good four-year program in, say, nursing, consult the staff at a *two-year* college. Their own school is out of the running, so they can give your question the impartial answer it deserves. If you do inquire at a college that you might ultimately attend, do not take the chairman's word for the quality of the program. Ask about the jobs students are offered and the graduate schools they attend.

Speak to friends who are back in college, particularly those in your own field. See whether they would choose the same school a second time, and why. Having friends at a college may not be the best reason for selecting it yourself, but it can't hurt to be guided by their experience.

Visiting Colleges

Take time to visit the colleges in your community, even if you are not planning to attend them. Just discovering the variety will open your eyes. Can you imagine yourself crammed into the elevator of a skyscraper college in the heart of town? Or sloshing your way across a suburban campus during a rainstorm? If a particular school unsettles you, decide why. Is it too big or too small, too bustling or too quiet? Does the noise in the student lounge set your teeth on edge? Does it bother you that the halls are a mess? You will be spending a lot of time in college; decide what you can and cannot live with.

Don't be sidetracked by features of no real interest to you, no matter how splendid. Concentrate on computer labs, child-care centers, studios, greenhouses—whatever *you* will need. The same approach applies to libraries. Compare them, not by popping into the reading room or checking the number of books, but by choosing an academic subject of particular interest to you—say, the French Revolution—and examining each college's resources in that one field.

Visit the departments in which you might enroll; faculty members can suggest pointers you might have overlooked. Even the bulletin boards can fill you in. Do the notices tell of professional meetings, or only that John needs a tutor and Mary wants to sell her books?

Above all, spend time with the students. Get them to talk about instructors, classmates, special facilities in their field. If ten students in a row tell you this college is the best thing that ever happened to them, you can end your search right there. But if all they volunteer is "Yeah . . . it's all right," find out why it isn't. Are the big-name professors too busy to talk to them? Is the library closed on Sundays, when they need it most? Are the renowned drama productions restricted to seniors majoring in theater?

Listen for good as well as bad. Yes, beginning courses are taught by part-timers, but they often explain things better than the regular faculty. It doesn't matter that cars are prohibited on campus; there's a free shuttle bus every ten minutes. Is the cafeteria mobbed? It's a sign that the food is good. A midtown campus may be short on glamour, but you can get there by public transportation.

Student observations must be taken for what they are worth. Some are isolated gripes. Some do not make any difference. But a few are eye-openers, highlighting the points that will or will not make college work for you.

The above suggestions will not identify the one perfect college for you. There is no such thing. You can probably learn happily and well on any of a dozen campuses, including several in your own community. Again, it comes down to setting priorities, weighing the trade-offs, and coming to grips with the key decisions.

STAGE 2: IDENTIFYING YOUR PRIORITIES

There is no shortage of colleges; just about any program you can imagine is offered somewhere in the country. The real question is: what's important to you?

Are you interested in a nontraditional program?
Are you interested in nontraditional features within a traditional program? Which ones?
What do you want to study?
Can an associate's degree be of use?
Which special features do you need? And why?
Do you plan to remain in your community, or are you free to relocate?

There are three thousand colleges in the United States. Your answers to these questions may narrow down the choice to three or four.

Nontraditional Programs

The two most common types of nontraditional program are the external degree program and the "limited-residence" program. In the first, you are never required to report on campus; there may not even be a campus. In the second, you are usually expected to register in person, attend an occasional seminar, or meet with an adviser every few weeks. Limited residence means that you must be close enough to manage the necessary visits; external degree programs allow you to live halfway around the world.

In either type, you can attend regular classes or replace them with a wide range of alternatives. You can earn independent study credit through projects you design yourself. You can sign up for correspondence courses employing anything from texts to television. You can explore the possibilities of summer study—perhaps combined with a vacation for the whole family. You can prepare for CLEP and ACT PEP exams. Or, if you prefer, you can enroll in conventional classes at any approved college and apply the credit to your nontraditional degree.

More structured external programs are also available. Instead of planning your own curriculum, you pursue one prepared by the college. You proceed course by course, as in any school, but all work is done by correspondence. Final examinations, taken under supervision in your own community, are part of the package. The approach works well for students who prefer a traditional, coordinated college program but cannot get to a campus.

External degree programs offer some compelling advantages—and a few drawbacks. Let's look at the positive side first.

> They are just about the least expensive programs you can find.
> They allow you to work at your own convenience in your own community. This makes them ideal for shut-ins, women with children, and students with job or family responsibilities.
> They enable you to earn college credit in whatever interests you. You might even earn credit for projects you would have undertaken anyway.
> They often grant maximum credit for prior learning.
> They allow you to progress at your own rate.
> There's rarely an admissions problem.

Your program is limited only by your own resources and imagination. If you want to summer in Maine and winter in Arizona, you are free to do so.

Limited-residence programs offer some of the same advantages. However, they may be more expensive; colleges usually charge their regular tuition and may also expect you to hire and pay an approved tutor to supervise your independent study. In addition, you will have to make trips to the campus. Moreover, many of these programs discourage formal classwork; the catalog of the University Without Walls refers explicitly to its students' "perception of exclusion from traditional university programs."

Now for the drawbacks.

When a field of study requires special equipment, working off-campus poses problems. Computer science calls for access to a large-scale computer. A physics course may require a fully equipped electronics lab. Physiology experiments could involve anything from a frog to a cadaver—nothing you'd want in your living room. The difficulties are not insurmountable. One student completed his lab courses as a nonmatriculated student at a university seventy-five miles away. Another made arrangements with a high school teacher. It can be done; it just requires an extra margin of energy and initiative.

The second problem runs deeper.

External degree programs put the responsibility for your education squarely on your own shoulders. They call for a certain type of person. A self-starter. A planner. Someone who will take the phone off the hook three nights a week because that's political science time. Fred Harvey Harrington, educational adviser to the Ford Foundation, warns of "the sense of loneliness that brings discouragement to adults working on their own." To some extent, you can take the edge off the difficulty by combining traditional classes with independent study. Nonetheless, the most successful external degree candidates are those who can maintain their enthusiasm and drive in the face of this intellectual isolation.

If you are not sure whether the approach is for you, try it on a small scale. Review the discussion of proficiency exams in chapter 7, and start preparing for a single exam. Set yourself a schedule and enlist the support of family and friends, just as you would in a more extensive program. Then see whether you sustain the effort. If you miss out, no harm has been done. If you persevere—if you find individual study tolerable, interesting, or even exciting—then you can reasonably consider a full-scale program.

But before committing yourself, you may want to ask one more question: how useful is an external degree? Researchers Carol P. Sosdian and Laure M. Sharp interviewed graduates of thirty-two external degree programs on their subsequent education or careers. They found that

> almost all those who sought access to higher-level academic programs were able to enroll. It is also clear that they did so in moderately selective institutions. . . . In the world of work, the external degree yielded tangible benefits for the majority of degree holders. Women as a group profited especially, as did those who were at the lower end of the occupational spectrum prior to degree completion.

However, this was at a time when the external degree was novel and glamorous. Over the next few years the tide may turn. Already, journalist Anne C. Roark, writing in the *Los Angeles Times*, notes that external degrees "raise enormous ethical and legal questions about the value of an academic degree." Although she was referring to degrees from nonaccredited private institutions, any challenge may tarnish even the most reputable program.

This suggests that if you are interested in an external degree, you look for a solid, established program at an accredited institution. Fashions in education come and go, but the degree you earn should be serviceable for the rest of your life.

The books listed earlier in this chapter mention up to 200 schools offering nontraditional degrees, many of them requiring little or no attendance on campus. However, a number of these schools are not accredited, or even interested in accreditation. Others have precarious futures for financial reasons. A few private colleges are so exclusively committed to nontraditional instruction that, should the field become overcrowded, they would have nothing to fall back on.

There are at least a half-dozen *inexpensive, accredited* public colleges offering external bachelor's degrees that require no campus visits at all. They include:

Indiana University
1125 East 38th Street, Room
    060
Indianapolis, IN 46205

Ohio University
Extension Division
Athens, OH 45701

Regents External Degree
    Program
University of the State of New
    York
Cultural Education Center
Albany, NY 12230

Thomas A. Edison College
1750 North Olden Avenue
Trenton, NJ 08638

University of Iowa
Inter-Institutional Program
Iowa City, IA 52242

University of Maryland
University College
College Park, MD 20742

Western Illinois University
Non-Traditional Programs
Macomb, IL 61455

Three of these, Ohio, Iowa, and Western Illinois, specialize in correspondence courses—although *any* external degree program will accept such courses, if they are from an accredited college. In addition, some states, including California, Florida, Missouri, and Ohio, provide their own external degree programs for residents; check with the state's higher education department when you are ready to begin.

In pinpointing these programs, we are not suggesting that they are best, either generally or in relation to your needs. Some offer only a limited range of subjects. Others require two years of study elsewhere before you can even enroll. A few specify a minimum time period for each course—say, a month—to ensure that you do justice to the material. So do not depend exclusively on this list; consult the appropriate directories to see whether other programs may serve you better. We provided these names only to demonstrate that in taking the external degree route, you need not settle for a questionable institution. You have plenty of stable, inexpensive accredited colleges to choose from.

We have been concentrating on the B.A. or B.S. degree, but most external programs also offer associate's degrees. If you need a high school diploma and cannot find a suitable program in your own community, Bronx Community College in New York offers an external program leading to the General Education Diploma, equivalent to a high school education. This may interest adults who do not want the whole town to know they never finished high school.

The picture is different on the graduate level. In the long run the value of a graduate degree may depend as much on the people you meet as on the content of your courses. The reputation of the program will also make a difference. Perhaps for these reasons, purely external, accredited graduate degree programs are uncommon in this country. The University of Alaska in Fairbanks offers degrees in geology and related subjects, but funding has been uncertain from year to year. Despite financial reverses, Antioch University in Yellow Springs, Ohio, still has master's programs in several fields. And the Consortium of California State Universities and Colleges (400 Golden Shore, Long Beach, CA 90802) sponsors graduate programs in education, social sciences, and the humanities for residents of the state.

If you can spend a few weeks on campus each year, the picture becomes brighter, with particularly good choices in education, business, and social science. Washington State University in Pullman has limited-residence programs in biology, computer science, and electrical engineering, and the Rochester Institute of Technology offers mathematics. If you are bent on an external or limited-residence graduate degree, check the references given earlier, but at the same time talk it over with faculty and others in your field.

Nontraditional Features Within Traditional Programs

External and limited-residence programs are at one extreme of the nontraditional spectrum. But as discussed in chapter 3, there are dozens of variations that can be combined with a conventional approach.

Here a good starting point is the *Chronicle Guide to External and Continuing Education*, mentioned earlier. The tables in this book provide college-by-college information covering such areas as

Evening and weekend courses
Off-campus courses
Credit for CLEP and similar examinations
Tuition
Freedom to design one's own program
External degree programs
Classroom study required for degree
Fields of study
Sources of further information

With so much ground to cover, this guide obviously cannot provide much more than a yes/no answer in each case. For more detailed information, try the following:

Evening and weekend programs. If you're like most students, you need an evening or weekend schedule because you have a nine-to-five job and cannot leave town anyway. You can dispense with large-scale research; just contact schools within commuting distance. Evening programs are offered at over a thousand colleges, so you shouldn't have too much trouble finding one. For weekend programs, check Wilbur Cross, *The Weekend Education Source Book* (New York: Harper's Magazine Press, 1976).

Vacation programs. Here a useful source is Gerson G. Eisenberg, *Learning Vacations* (Baltimore, Md.: Eisenberg Educational Enterprises, 1980). Eisenberg lists educational programs offered in America, abroad, or en route. Some are sponsored by recognized colleges and carry college credit. In other cases you may be able to receive credit at your school by requesting a challenge examination on what you have learned.

Don't overlook the conventional summer classes offered at most large metropolitan colleges—assuming, of course, that the credit you earn can be transferred to your own school. Programs usually run from three to six weeks, with a particularly good selection of courses at the introductory level. If you live out of town and are worried about the cost of living in the city, give a thought to house swapping with friends or friends of friends. But do not make final arrangements until you are sure of being admitted; most colleges give priority to their own students. (By the same token, your chances of acceptance are increased if you keep an open mind about what you are willing to study.) For further details, write directly to the colleges in which you are interested.

Cooperative education programs. These programs enable you to combine classroom study with practical supervised experience in your field. You are paid at the going rate for the type of work; earnings can reach several thousand dollars a year. A complete list of coop education programs appears in *Undergraduate Programs of Cooperative Education in the United States and Canada,* available from the National Commission for Cooperative Education, 360

Huntington Avenue, Boston, MA 02115. The 563 senior colleges and 484 junior colleges listed in the 1980 edition probably include several in your own community. Fields include just about anything you could want: agriculture and related areas, fine and applied art, business, computer science, education, engineering, health professions, humanities, mathematics, natural and social sciences, performing arts, technology and trade, or industrial skills. More than half the colleges recognize the value of your off-campus work by granting regular college credit, applicable toward the degree.

Correspondence and television courses. What takes place in a correspondence course? You complete a lesson, mail in your assignment, get it back with corrections and a grade, and move on to the next lesson, just as in any class. The difference is that you learn primarily from printed materials, sometimes supplemented by audiotape, television, and other resources.

Most guides to nontraditional education include correspondence courses. For more detailed information, check *Guide to Independent Study Through Correspondence Instruction 1980–1982,* available from Peterson's Guides, NUEA Book Order Department, P.O. Box 978, Edison, NJ 08817. Not only does this source list 69 accredited colleges offering correspondence courses, with information on eligibility and costs, but it goes on to describe the courses themselves—12,000 of them, with name, department, level of instruction, and credits for each.

Home television study is a variation on correspondence courses, with TV provided as an additional learning resource. A good way to find out what is available is to contact your local TV stations, both cable and regular. The people in charge may not be education experts, but they know what is being transmitted in your area.

Alternatively, the material may be available on videotape. Although only a handful of colleges offer videotape for home use— the playback equipment is still something of a novelty—an increasing number provide video-based courses that you can watch at a learning center, on or off campus. In the forefront are the University of Maryland in College Park, the University of Minnesota in Minneapolis, the City Colleges of Chicago, and the University of

Southern Illinois at Edwardsville. As yet, there is no central clearinghouse for such programs, but you can get some information from:

Corporation for Public Broadcasting
1111 16th Street NW
Washington, DC 20036

British Open University Foundation
110 East 59th Street
New York, NY 10022

Self-paced courses. These were mentioned in chapter 5. Typically, you report to a campus learning center, but instead of attending conventional lectures, you study at your own pace from printed, audiovisual, or computer resources. (Even attending the center may be optional, if you can learn without it.) For students whose learning style leans toward independence and who have the discipline to work without outside prodding, self-paced courses can be a delight. For help in tracking them down, write to the Center for Personalized Instruction, Georgetown University, Washington, DC 20057.

Independent study. Even in traditional programs, virtually all colleges allow you to earn some credits—usually between fifteen and thirty— by planning and carrying out a project of your own. If you want to do more independent study than that, you might as well enroll in a nontraditional program.

What Are You Planning to Study?

For some returning adults, field of study is the single most important factor in choosing a college. For others, it does not matter at all.

Laura is a secretary in the local Social Security office. She is interested in a range of higher-level openings that require a bachelor's degree—any bachelor's degree. Field of study does not even enter into Laura's choice of college; she will probably continue with her original major, simply to save time.

Dale has had a taste of computer science at work and wants to learn everything there is to know about it. Even for Dale, field of study will not affect his choice of college, as over a thousand campuses now offer a program in computer science.

Like Dale, Elizabeth is positive about her field: women's studies. Unfortunately, only thirteen colleges offer it as a major, and the closest of them is 700 miles away.

Field of study affects your choice of college only if you are in Elizabeth's position: first, you know exactly what you want to study, and second, it's available on relatively few campuses.

Several directories list college majors and the school where each is offered. They also indicate the level at which you can work—certificate, associate's degree, bachelor's, master's, or doctorate.

In organizing the information, two different systems are used. Some directories, including the *College Blue Book: Degrees Offered by College and Subject* (New York: The Macmillan Co., 1981), have all majors in a single, strictly alphabetical list. This makes them easy to find; if you are interested in horticulture, you just look it up. On the other hand, you might not think of checking such closely related entries as Environmental Horticulture, Landscape Horticulture, or even Forestry. They are all in the book but not where you are most likely to come upon them.

The other system, used by the *College Handbook Index of Majors* (New York: College Entrance Examination Board, 1981), arranges fields into broad categories such as Education, Health Science, and Foreign Languages. Related subjects appear together within these categories. Thus, Horticulture, Ornamental Horticulture, and Agricultural and Farm Management are on consecutive pages under *Agriculture;* Landscape Horticulture does not appear at all. Both systems are fine, but in the first, be sure to identify related entries that overlap your original one.

Sometimes a preferred field of study may narrow down your choice of a college to zero. Harvey is interested in medical illustration, but the degree is offered by only four colleges, all of them ruled out for other reasons. What options are open to him?

Quite a few. He can major in art, with a strong minor in anatomy. Or develop his own interdisciplinary major, combining the two fields. He might earn credit through independent study, possibly under the auspices of a local hospital. Or choose an external degree built around his specialty.

If, like Harvey, you cannot get to the college that offers your major, consider a related field. If dance therapy is available on only two campuses in the whole country, try physical therapy. Not one college offers a bachelor's degree in culinary arts, but you can study the same material by enrolling as a dietetics major.

If you have relatively few credits, there is another alternative. Complete your required and introductory courses at the most convenient college (or by independent study) and hope that when you are ready to specialize a few years from now, things will be brighter. By that time the major you want may be more readily available. The loan and grant picture may improve, particularly if you maintain good grades. Perhaps you can save enough for a year or two at the college of your choice. It's even possible that your interests will change. Finishing up your introductory work looks like a stalling operation, but it makes sense.

Should you return to the major you originally chose? That depends. If you have lost interest, then forget it. Otherwise, think it over in light of the person you are today. Will the field meet your needs for both intellectual challenge and career opportunities? Is it realistic in terms of your own strengths and weaknesses? Was the work originally more difficult, painstaking, or tedious than you had expected? Could it have played a part in your decision to leave school? If you still retain your original enthusiasm, try a couple of courses. But if you associate the field with earlier frustration and disappointment, choose a new one even if it means sacrificing some credits.

Finally, if you cannot decide on a major, consider a degree in general studies or liberal arts, already available on more than fifty campuses throughout the country.

Can an Associate's Degree Help You?

We have seen that the community college offers technical and career programs not available elsewhere. In addition, for students with qualms about their academic abilities, it serves as an excellent transition to the more stringent demands of the four-year college. It will get you back into the swing of paying attention in class, preparing for exams, or researching and writing a paper. It often provides guidance, child care, remediation, and special schedules for returning adults. On top of that the community college is *affordable*—an A.A. at a municipal two-year college can save you thousands of dollars. And if, at some point, you decide to interrupt your studies, the associate's degree is a generally accepted place to take a break.

This is no guarantee that a two-year college is right for you. Many students prefer to settle into a four-year college at once rather than go through the admissions procedure a second time. Some community colleges have a residence requirement, which might mean losing credits if you are already a sophomore. If you are much past that, you probably have as many introductory courses as you can use. In any case, attending too many colleges can make you look like a bad risk.

Which Special Features Do You Need—and Why?

Back in chapter 4, we looked at reasons for returning to college. Do you need a degree? Do you need some particular knowledge or skills, with or without a degree? Or are you returning for other reasons of your own?

Your answers to these questions define your rock-bottom priorities. But there is more to college than rock-bottom priorities. You're investing a lot in college. In return, you deserve, not only the bare bones of an education, but some of the extras you associate with returning to school. We are not denying the distinction between essentials on the one hand and preferences on the other. We are cautiously suggesting that each may have its place.

Lois is examining colleges in the Southwest because her doctor thinks the climate may help her chronic bronchitis. For Lois this is an urgent personal need. Cheryl, returning to school after a four-year hiatus, is also considering colleges in the Southwest. She dropped out in the first place because for seven months of the year her campus was covered with slush and snow; she hated even to get out of bed. This time she's heading straight for the Sunbelt. Is Cheryl indulging herself? No. Cheryl's psychological needs may be every bit as real as Lois's physical ones. Her goal is to finish college.

Anything that helps—or that she thinks will help—is worth considering.

Obviously there are some hard-core needs. An astronomy major requires access to an observatory. Video production calls for equipment and a studio. If you have young children, a child-care center has high priority.

These are necessities. But now let's look at some of the "extras."

With a forty-hour job, Tim is looking for a part-time program. But he's a morning person, up at six and with his best work done by noon. Late-evening courses would demolish him. Tim needs a weekend program, even if it narrows down his choice of college to one.

Leo finds that tall buildings and crowded streets make him uncomfortable. It's irrational, he'll have to come to terms with it someday, but meanwhile it's a fact. He's considering only schools on the outskirts of town.

Paula's problem, if that is the word, was that she first saw the state college campus in the magical, rosy light of a September sunset and promptly fell in love with the place. Courses and credits are part of life, but so is love. With everyone arguing against it, Paula enrolled anyway and never regretted it. She graduated last spring with a record that astonished everybody, including herself.

Identifying your preferences is no guarantee that you will be able to get them. But that's no reason for pooh-poohing them in the first place. Individual reactions may be irrational, but that doesn't make them less real. They're as much a part of you as your choice of major. Make life easier by taking them into account.

Do You Plan to Remain in Your Own Community?

Reentry adults often have families and jobs. Whatever the charms of colleges around the country, they are staying right where they are. Because 99 percent of the possibilities are ruled out, they can do a thorough job on the remainder.

If this describes you, get a local map, decide how far you can commute, and track down all the colleges within that range. There may be more than you think. Don't overlook schools in the next state; they may be closer than some in your own county.

Reread the pertinent descriptions in the college catalog. A few schools will immediately be eliminated because of costs, entrance requirements, schedules, or course offerings. Visit the rest, preferably at the time of day you would actually be attending. First impressions are important; if something about a college puts you off, it probably is not the one for you.

Talk to people in the community. Sharon found three nursing programs within a radius of forty miles. While applying to all three, she also spoke to her doctor and his nurse-receptionist, to employment offices at the local hospital, and to some friends in the health field. As a result, she ruled out one school altogether and chose between the others on the basis of cost. On a wider scale this would have been impossible; it was easy in her own community.

Now a few don'ts. Don't settle on a college merely because it is the first one you ever heard of. Or because you were thinking of going there two years ago. Or because your friend is going (although that may contribute!). Or because it is nearest. By the same token, don't pass up a college because you know nothing about it; find out. If several local colleges are part of the same state or municipal system, don't assume they are all the same. On the contrary, they may differ in everything that matters, including philosophy, programs, and admissions policies. That's why there's more than one in the first place.

Even if no college in the area seems exactly right, don't give up. At least a half-dozen external degree programs are open to you, and other programs may require your presence no more than once or twice a month.

STAGE 3: HOMING IN

By now we have considered various features of different college programs and how to find out who offers them. Except for costs, which are discussed in the next chapter, the remaining step is to re-examine your priorities and home in. Are you determined to major in cultural anthropology even if it means moving three states away? Are you willing to quit your job and take a loan to attend college full-time—and have you broken the news to your family?

Chances are that in some respects you have no choice; circumstances have locked you in. Don't fight it. If you cannot go to college out of town, go in town. If you cannot go days, go evenings. If you were bent on studying medicine until your second D in biochemistry, look for some other health-related career. Keep going. The difference between any degree and none at all is vastly greater than the difference between one degree and another.

Can You Get In?

Somewhere—yes. Everywhere—no.

The college acceptance rat race is over. A 1978 study covering more than half the colleges in the country showed an acceptance rate of 83 percent. A third of the colleges, including 28 percent of the senior colleges, described themselves as "open door." Most were recruiting actively; nearly half were recruiting adults. The picture looks good.

You know where you stand. You know your academic record and your standardized test scores. Match your own qualifications with those of the schools you have in mind. But bear in mind that here, as elsewhere in college, there is always room for special cases.

Many colleges have separate criteria for minorities, women, students from disadvantaged backgrounds, and athletes. A woman turned down for a literature program may be accepted into a male-dominated field like engineering. The same is true of men in education or nursing. A relatively weak score on the verbal part of a standardized test may be offset by a dazzling one in mathematics. In some programs age may count against you; in others, you won't even be considered unless you are over twenty-five.

Will a personal interview help? You are the best judge. If you do go this route, be cautious. Think of your interviews as business talks, not therapy sessions. Tell the truth, but don't say anything for which you will kick yourself afterward. If you licked your drug problem five years ago, why mention it at all? If you depended heavily on the frat house's collection of past exams, so did a lot of other people. Do not be seduced by the fact that the interviewer across the desk seems really interested; it's part of the job. Your part is to present yourself in the best possible light, as effectively as you can. Hold back on information that could hurt you.

Colleges are flexible. A low SAT score may be outweighed by strong transcripts, and vice versa. The essays and backgrounds of returning adults may offset any academic considerations. Even specific admissions requirements have been waived. Maybe the college simply needs someone from your part of the country.

So if you have your heart set on a particular college and you think you have a chance, go ahead and apply. Make as good a case as you can, but do not expect the admissions office to be so enchanted with your candor that they will let you in no matter what. Have a few "safeties" ready in the wings.

Study the Catalogs

Once you have narrowed your choices to a few schools, you will learn more from their catalogs than from any other source. Theoretically, students must conform to the procedures described in the catalog. If you have overlooked a prerequisite, if you neglect to withdraw properly from a course, if you violate the honor code, the administration can always defend itself with the simple words, "It's in the catalog."

Turn the pages and see what applies to you. Watch for admissions procedures, required courses, majors, student rights and regulations, special services, extracurricular activities. See if there are separate tuition schedules for full- and part-time students, and how you can benefit. Glance at the list of honors and awards—did you know that some long-dead alumnus has provided an annual prize of $500 for the best essay on the electoral college?

Read in detail the section on your own department. Find the names of the chairman and the faculty adviser. Which courses are required? Which are recommended? How often are they scheduled? If essential courses are offered only every other year, the department may be too small to serve your purpose.

While you are browsing, look for a map of the campus or a discussion of parking regulations. Take notes on potential problems. These are the ones you will want to iron out before making any final decisions.

Talk over Your Plans with Family and Friends

If you are in class three nights a week, your spouse's social life will be affected. Your weekend courses may double someone else's burden of chores. The decision to take a loan and attend college full-time is not between you and yourself; it affects everyone who will be scrimping to pay it back. If no one is dependent on you and vice versa, you are free to steer your own course. Otherwise, the people who are affected by your decisions have a right to share in them.

This means talking it over, defining the alternatives, and coming to joint conclusions. It goes far beyond muttering one morning, as you dash off to work, "By the way . . . that weekend program at the community college is beginning to look good." Discussing plans will reveal difficulties in time to do something about them. Perhaps you can take the children with you to weekend classes and leave them in the day-care center. Maybe you should take a room at that out-of-town college and come home weekends—a shaky arrangement but sometimes workable. Or you could complete the first two years of college at a nearby school and save the big move for your junior year.

If you fail to talk over your plans with those around you, they will become furious and miserable by turns. Both conditions are contagious; it will be only a matter of time before you show the symptoms yourself. Talk things over in advance—not merely in the interest of justice and fair play, but to provide the peace of mind you will need to get on with your work.

Contact the College

If, with all your investigating, you still have misgivings, questions, or unresolved problems, take your concerns to the appropriate college office.

We have already mentioned the advisability of contacting campuses to find out about before-credits. Other areas of concern may include the following:

Class schedules. Because of your own responsibilities, you may be able to attend courses only during certain hours, or on certain days of the week. Check with the dean of students or the admissions office to determine whether this can be arranged.

Required courses. Bear in mind that required courses can be totally rewarding, particularly if they are in a new field. This having been said, there may still be occasions when you want out.

Some colleges officially waive gym requirements for adults; others do it unofficially. If your foreign language skills were wretched and have become worse, find out whether you can substitute a European literature course conducted in English. If you have been involved with music for a decade and doubt whether you will learn anything new from a required introductory course, check that out, too. Thousands of returning adults have taken required courses, however reluctantly, and been glad in the end. But if you foresee difficulties, contact the department or the office of student affairs ahead of time.

Prerequisites. Sometimes you are really looking forward to a course, only to discover that you don't have the prerequisites. If you are willing to chance it anyway, contact the department. In such fields as mathematics and science, bypassing prerequisites is hazardous even if permission is granted. In the humanities and the social sciences, your own reading and background may more than compensate for a missing course or two.

Job opportunities. For students who expect to work, an on-campus job can save hours of travel time and provide a congenial environment in the bargain. While routine jobs are usually filled by work-study students, there are often openings for typists, lab assistants, tutors, word processors, cashiers—anyone with a specific, marketable skill. Working full-time may even entitle you to free tuition. Check with the college's personnel department and the student employment office.

Withdrawing from classes. Phil signed up for nine credits, only to be transferred across country by his company six weeks later. Clara had to withdraw because of family illness. Olga left because her son had trouble adjusting to her absence.

What happens if you leave college before the end of the semester? Must you withdraw from all courses, or can you finish a couple on your own? Is there a deadline for tuition refunds? A penalty if your work has been below C? This may never be your problem, but it helps to get the facts in advance.

Accreditation. This was mentioned in chapter 4. If you have any lingering doubts about the accreditation of the college itself or the certification of the program you are after, resolve them now.

The college is there to help you. If you have any last lingering doubts, let them know.

Should You Return to Your Original School?

Returning to your original school has a lot to recommend it.

Let's assume that practical matters like cost, location, and major field pose no problems. Now ask yourself why you left in the first place.

Maybe it *was* the wrong school: too big, too impersonal, too demanding. But would any college have served you better in those days? Or were you simply not in a college frame of mind?

If you are convinced that you hate the place, always did, and always will, then forget it. Otherwise, your earlier reasons for enrolling may still apply: good faculty, strong program, convenient campus. You will get as much credit for prior course work as you would anywhere. You'll come in knowing your way around.

One thing you may be sure of. The handful of people who may remember you won't hold grudges. On the contrary, they will welcome you back with honest goodwill. It takes courage and determination to return, and they know it. You forgive them; they forgive you. In a month you'll be wondering what could have gone wrong in the first place.

So don't rule out your original school. There have been a lot of changes since you were nineteen.

Educational Brokering

Educational brokers are matchmakers, pairing students with colleges. They have on file a wealth of information about educational programs throughout the area. You tell them what you need and they find a match. As a rule they are nonprofit, receiving support from foundations, government grants, or other agencies. They are usually based outside of colleges, because an office associated with a particular school is not likely to be impartial. Don't confuse them with commercial, profit-making school advisory services, which receive a cash payment for each recruit and may not put *your* interests first.

But educational brokers are no substitute for thinking through what you need or want. If you yourself are vague about your requirements, they can help put things in focus. In general, the more information you can provide about your needs, the more effectively they can serve you.

Educational brokering is still a novel idea. New offices open; sometimes old ones close for lack of funds. To obtain a directory of reputable brokers, send $4.00 to the National Committee for Educational Brokering, 1211 Connecticut Avenue NW, Washington, DC 20036.

There's just one more stumbling block, and it's a big one. It's known as money. That is what chapter 9 is all about.

Nine

Paying Your Way

That college costs money is hardly news. Let's see how much money we're talking about.

Tuition at many private colleges is now over $6,000 a year; room and board can bring the figure to $10,000 or more. Tuition at state colleges is about $2,000 for out-of-state students, and drops to as little as $300 for state residents. CLEP examinations cost about $25 each—under $9.00 a credit—while a Regents External Degree taken entirely by examination may be as low as $450 *altogether;* if you come in with transfer credit, it may be even less.

To be sure, college costs go far beyond tuition. They include fees, books, transportation, supplies, and such individual expenses as child care, room and board, or extra meals away from home.

Keeping costs down is not the only way to balance the budget. We have already noted that college funds are often made available, on the basis not of total cost, but of "financial need," the *difference* between what your education will cost and what you can afford to pay. So the most exclusive private university—assuming you can get in—may cost no more than the municipal two-year college across the street. On the other hand, merely proving financial need is no assurance that you will get what you require. Most scholarship and loan programs have a maximum, and often the colleges themselves, much as they would like to help you, simply don't have the funds.

Nonetheless, as a reentry student you may finance your studies through a variety of public and private channels. Even if you can pay your own way, it is usually worthwhile to investigate outside sources of funding; at the very least, you may be eligible for a guaranteed loan at a favorable rate of interest.

You needn't be an outstanding student to qualify for financial aid. You needn't attend full-time. Nor must you be near the poverty line; some benefits are available regardless of financial need, while others define need so liberally that you may qualify even if your family income is $50,000 a year or more.

What you *do* require are promptness and perseverance. The sooner you learn about sources of funding, the more likely you are to benefit. For students entering college in September, many scholarship and loan applications should be submitted the previous fall—nearly a year in advance! But you should start to collect information even earlier. In short, the ideal time to begin reading up on financial aid is eighteen to twenty months before you plan to begin classes.

The effort can be rewarding. If you spend fifty hours applying for aid and receive $1,500 the first year, your rate of pay is $30 an hour. It goes even higher if your benefits continue for a second or third year. So brace yourself and get started. Do not decide on your own that you "don't stand a chance" at some particular funding agency. Once you determine that you are eligible, present yourself in the best possible light and let *them* do the deciding.

As you read this section, keep stationery and stamps handy. When you come across the name of an agency you want to contact, send out a letter at once. Make a copy of every piece of correspondence, including the date; here some old-fashioned carbon paper may be useful.

You will want some photocopies of your last few tax returns. These are needed for two reasons: to confirm your financial circumstances, and to establish that you are an "independent student"—that is, someone supported primarily by yourself or your spouse, in contrast to a "dependent student," supported chiefly by parents or guardian. If you are under thirty, you may also need copies of your parents' returns, to show that you were not claimed as a dependent.

Financial aid takes a variety of forms. Most attractive are *scholarships and grants*, which do not have to be repaid. *Loans* are repaid, but often not until after graduation, and then at a favorable rate of interest. Inflation also adds to the value of a low-interest loan; the $1,000 you borrow today may seem like a lot less when you have to repay it several years from now. *Tuition remission* funds never go through your hands at all; they are applied directly to the cost of tuition. Under a *tuition refund plan*, favored by many employers, you pay for your courses yourself and are reimbursed in whole or part as you complete them. *Part-time employment*, also known as *work-study*, may be part of the financial aid package your college offers you. And in *cooperative education*, described in chapter 3, the money you earn during periods of employment may cover your expenses for the entire year.

You can also think of financial aid as *unrestricted* or *restricted*. Restricted programs are limited to special groups such as veterans, women, and members of ethnic minorities. Unrestricted aid can be considered by any student.

Who supplies all this money? It can come from a variety of sources.

> *Personal.* This includes your own earnings and savings, as well as gifts or loans from family or friends.
>
> *Governmental.* Federal or state programs may provide grants, loans, or part-time jobs. In addition, restricted funds are available for veterans, the physically handicapped, financially disadvantaged, and so on.
>
> *College funds.* Here the college itself finances your loan, grant, or part-time employment.
>
> *Company or union benefits* related to your work.
>
> *Private agencies.* There are thousands of these, including churches, foundations, corporations, private trusts, professional organizations, and nonprofit agencies devoted to minorities, women, the handicapped, and so on.

One thing you can count on: applying for financial aid means filling out forms. The most widely used are the Financial Aid Form (FAF) and the Family Financial Statement (FFS), either of which can be used to apply for federal, state, and college aid with a single application. Your college will tell you which it prefers. Pennsylvania and California have prepared their own forms, for use at public colleges within the state. In addition, the federal government distributes Basic Grant forms, used to apply for the very popular Pell grants (formerly known as Basic Education Opportunity Grants, or BEOG); during the academic year 1981/82, an estimated 2.7 million students received these grants, averaging about $900 each.

As a rule, the college financial aid office provides the forms you need, along with information on completing them. Don't let the forms rattle you. Admittedly, you cannot dash them off during TV commercials. However, if you line up your financial information in advance, and then allow a couple of hours, they won't pose any problems. A typical Basic Grants form appears on pages 132 and 133. It is even shorter than it looks, since it includes separate sections for dependent and independent students.

The college will also provide a timetable for the return of completed forms. Please take that timetable *very* seriously. Financial aid deadlines are strict; a delay of a single day could cost you hundreds of dollars. Forms must usually be processed well in advance of enrollment, although Pell grants are an exception; you can apply for them even after classes start.

The best place to start your search for funds is a college financial aid office. Even if your plans are still indefinite, talk with financial aid advisers on the nearest campus. Ask for information both on unrestricted aid programs and on any restricted programs that may apply to you. Once your college applications have been submitted, you can obtain more specific information from the schools you are considering.

However, if you want to begin researching on your own, here are some suggestions. Unrestricted programs are covered first, restricted programs follow.

Federal Programs

Federal aid is volatile. Every day new changes are proposed. Some are implemented; others are turned down. If you want your full share of federal funds, it is essential to keep abreast of these developments. Read the newspapers. Establish contact with the nearest office of your congressman and senator—or write them directly in Washington. For current information on federal financial aid, call the toll-free number 800-638-6700 from 9 A.M. to 6 P.M., Eastern time (Maryland residents call 800-492-6602). If you keep getting a busy signal, try your college's financial aid office. We don't want to scare you, but trying to get this year's money by last year's rules is a losing battle.

In the fall of 1981, the federal government had six financial aid programs based chiefly on need. In all cases you must carry at least six credits at an approved institution or external degree program, and be working toward a degree or certificate.

Two grant programs, Pell grants and Supplemental Education Opportunity Grants (SEOG), are based on financial need and course load, and are available only to undergraduates. You can apply for a Pell grant through your college or on your own; forms can be obtained from financial aid offices or by writing to Federal Student Aid Programs, Box 84, Washington, DC 20044. SEOG is administered by the individual college; apply through the financial aid office.

Three loan programs are available to both undergraduates and graduate students. *Guaranteed Student Loans* are issued by banks or other lending institutions. The interest rate is moderate (9 percent in 1982) and is paid by the government until nine months after you leave school. Financial need is not an issue unless your family income is over $30,000 a year. However, lining up the loan is your responsibility, and it may not be easy. (Your financial aid office may have some suggestions.) Start with your own bank and then branch out; allow plenty of time. Finding a loan is a little like job hunting; you get plenty of *nos*, but all you need is one *yes*. Around 3 million students qualify each year, so it can't be hopeless.

Auxiliary Loans to Assist Students are similar to Guaranteed Student Loans. The interest rate is higher (14 percent in 1981) but so is the income ceiling; households with incomes as high as $100,-000 a year are eligible if several members are attending expensive private colleges. Again, locating the loan is up to you.

National Direct Student Loans are intended for low-income students who could not otherwise remain in college. The interest rate is only 4 percent. Funds come from the government or college,

Basic Grant
Application Form

School Year 1981-82
Read instructions as you fill out this form.

WARNING: If you use this form to establish your eligibility for Federal student aid funds, you should know that any person who makes false statements or misrepresentations on this form is subject to a fine or to imprisonment or both, under provisions of the United States Criminal Code.

U.S. DEPARTMENT OF EDUCATION

FORM APPROVED
FEDAC NO. H 94
APP. EXP. 6/82

No grant may be awarded unless a completed application form has been received (20 USC 1070a (b) (2)).

Section A Student's Information

1. Student's name
   Last | First | M.I.

2. Student's permanent mailing address
   (see page 3 for State abbreviation)
   Number and Street
   City | State | Zip Code

3. Student's social security number

4. Student's date of birth
   Month Day Year

5. Student's State of legal residence
   State

Fold 6. The student is
   (a) ☐ a U.S. citizen
   (b) ☐ an eligible noncitizen (see instructions)
   (c) ☐ neither of the above (see instructions)

7. The student is
   ☐ unmarried (single, divorced, or widowed)
   ☐ married
   ☐ separated

8. Student's year in college during 1981-82
   ☐ 1st (freshman)
   ☐ 2nd (sophomore)
   ☐ 3rd (junior)
   ☐ 4th (senior)
   ☐ 5th (undergraduate)
   ☐ graduate or professional (beyond a Bachelor's degree)

9. Will the student have a Bachelor's degree by July 1, 1981?
   ☐ Yes (see instructions)
   ☐ No

Fold

Section B Student's Status

Read the instructions to find out who counts as the student's parent before you answer 10, 11, and 12.

	Yes No	Yes No
10. Did or will the student live with the parents for more than six weeks	. . . in 1980? ☐ ☐	. . . in 1981? ☐ ☐
11. Did or will the parents claim the student as an income tax exemption	. . . in 1980? ☐ ☐	. . . in 1981? ☐ ☐
12. Did or will the student get more than $1,000 worth of support from the parents	. . . in 1980? ☐ ☐	. . . in 1981? ☐ ☐

If you answered "Yes" to any of the questions in Section B, you must fill in the blue shaded areas. If your parents are separated or divorced, if your parent is widowed, or if you have a stepparent, you must read the instructions on page 4 before going on. **Don't** fill in the gray shaded areas.

If you answered "No" to all 6 questions in Section B, you must fill in the gray shaded areas. Don't fill in the blue shaded areas.

Section C Household Information

Parents

13. The parents' current marital status is
   ☐ single   ☐ divorced   ☐ widowed
   ☐ married   ☐ separated

14. The parents' State of legal residence is

15. The age of the older parent is

Student (& spouse)

18. The total size of the student's household during 1981-82 will be
   Include the student, spouse, and student's dependent children. Include other dependents if they meet the definition in the instructions.

16. The total size of the parents' household during 1981-82 will be
   Include the student even if he/she does not live at home. Include parents and parents' other dependent children. Include other dependents if they meet the definition in the instructions.

17. Of the number in 16, how many will be in college during 1981-82?
   Include the student who is applying for aid and others who will be in college at least half-time.

19. Of the number in 18, how many will be in college during 1981-82?
   Include the student who is applying for aid and others who will be in college at least half-time.

Section D Income and Expense Information

	Parents	Student (& spouse)
20. A 1980 U.S. income tax return will be filed or has been filed	20. ☐ Yes ☐ No	20. ☐ Yes ☐ No

If you answered "Yes" to 20, go to 21. If you answered "No" to 20, skip to 26.

Tax Filers Only

21. The following 1980 U.S. income tax return figures are . . . . (see instructions)	21. ☐ from a completed return ☐ estimated	21. ☐ from a completed return ☐ estimated
22. 1980 total number of exemptions (Form 1040, line 7 or 1040A, line 6)	22.	22.
23. 1980 IRS Adjusted Gross Income (Form 1040, line 31 or 1040A, line 11) (see instructions)	23. $ .00	23. $ .00
24. 1980 U.S. income tax paid (Form 1040, line 47 or 1040A, line 14a)	24. $ .00	24. $ .00
25. 1980 itemized deductions (Form 1040, Schedule A, line 39, or write "0" if deductions were not itemized)	25. $ .00	25. $ .00

ED FORM 255

Section D (continued on other side)

Section D (continued)

	Parents	Student (& spouse)
26. 1980 income earned from work by . . . . 26a. Father	$ .00	26a. Student $ .00
26b. Mother	$ .00	26b. Spouse $ .00
27. 1980 nontaxable income		
a. Social security benefits (Parents: Include the student's benefits. See instructions.)	$ .00	27a. $ .00
b. Aid to Families with Dependent Children (AFDC or ADC)	$ .00	27b. $ .00
c. Other nontaxable income (Use the worksheet in the instructions.)	$ .00	27c. $ .00
28. 1980 medical and dental expenses not paid by insurance	$ .00	28. $ .00
29. 1980 elementary, junior high, and high school tuition paid (Don't include tuition paid for the student.)	$ .00	29. $ .00
30. Expected 1981 taxable and nontaxable income (See instructions.)	$ .00	

If you are filling in the gray shaded areas, skip to Section E. Don't answer 30, 31, and 32.

If you are filling in the blue shaded areas, answer 31 and 32 about the student. Use the worksheets in the instructions to figure out the answers.

31. Student's (& spouse's) total 1980 income minus U.S. income tax paid	$ .00
32. Student's (& spouse's) savings and net assets	$ .00

Section E Asset Information

	Parents		Student (& spouse)	
	What is it worth now?	What is owed on it?	What is it worth now?	What is owed on it?
33. Cash, savings, and checking accounts	$ .00		$ .00	
34. Home	$ .00	$ .00	$ .00	$ .00
35. Other real estate and investments	$ .00	$ .00	$ .00	$ .00
36. Business and farm	$ .00	$ .00	$ .00	$ .00

All students must fill in Sections F and G.

Section F Student's (& spouse's) Expected Income

July 1, 1981—June 30, 1982

37. Social security benefits (Include only the student's benefits.)
Amount per month $ .00   Number of months ☐☐

38. Veterans educational benefits (Include only the student's benefits from the GI Bill and Dependents Educational Assistance Program. Don't include the new VA Contributory Benefits.)
Amount per month $ .00   Number of months ☐☐

39. Other nontaxable income of student (& spouse)
(Don't include student financial aid or any of the benefits given in 37 and 38.)
Amount for July 1, 1981—June 30, 1982 $ .00

	Summer 1981	School Year 1981-82
40. a. Student's taxable income (Don't include student financial aid.)	3 months $ .00	9 months $ .00
b. Spouse's taxable income (Don't include student financial aid.)	3 months $ .00	9 months $ .00

Section G Colleges, Release, and Certification

41. Student's college for the 1981-82 school year

1. _____
Name of College

_____
City   State

2. _____
Name of College

_____
City   State

Basic Grant use only ☐☐☐ ☐☐☐

42. I give the Basic Grant Program permission to send information from this form to:

a. the financial aid agency in my State ☐ Yes ☐ No

b. the colleges I listed in 41 ☐ Yes ☐ No

See the instructions. If you leave (a) or (b) blank, we will count your answer as "No." If you answer "No" to (a), your State aid may be delayed.

43. Certification

All the information on this form is true and complete to the best of my(our) knowledge. If asked by an authorized official, I(we) agree to give proof of the information that I(we) have given on this form. I(We) realize that this proof may include a copy of my(our) 1980 U.S. or State income tax return. I(We) also realize that if I(we) do not give proof when asked, the student may not get aid.

Sign:
_____
Student

_____
Student's Spouse

_____
Father

_____
Mother

Date completed ☐☐ ☐☐ ☐☐
Month Day Year

Mail your form to:
Basic Grants
P.O. Box 92781
Los Angeles, CA 90009

not a bank, so locating a loan is not an issue. Apply directly to your college's financial aid office.

College Work-Study programs, open to undergraduates and graduate students, provide part-time employment on the basis of financial need. Although the rate of pay is close to the legal minimum, these programs have one important advantage: you can usually arrange your hours around your regular classes. Work-study programs are administered by the individual college, so again, apply to the financial aid office.

We repeat: Federal programs change rapidly. Any printed information may be out of date by the time you read it. To get all the federal aid you're entitled to, keep informed through the channels mentioned earlier: newspapers, federal legislators, the school's financial aid office, and the toll-free numbers listed above.

State Programs

Nearly all states have their own financial aid programs. You can get details by contacting your financial aid office or by writing to the address given in Appendix 3. Be sure to ask whether part-time students are eligible and whether aid is based on being a resident of the state, attending college there, or both. If you are already a resident, writing to your state legislators may be worthwhile. (You can get their names from the League of Women Voters.) Because legislators are in business to help their constituents, you may receive all sorts of useful information along with the answers to your questions.

College Programs

In 1981 *The Chronicle of Higher Education* reported that "at institutions charging more than $4500, 42.6 percent of the aid for freshmen comes from institutional funds." Almost all colleges have their own programs, ranging from small emergency loans to full scholarships. Some information can be found in the college catalog; for further details contact the financial aid office. Ask about specific features of interest to you, such as child care, textbook funds, free individual tutoring, or help for the handicapped.

On the graduate level, look into fellowships, assistantships, and tuition waivers. These may be available even to part-time stu-

dents when grades and recommendations warrant it. Discuss the
possibilities with the university's financial aid office and the department chairman in your field.

Company and Union Benefits

Among companies with more than 500 employees, 89 percent provide some sort of tuition aid; smaller firms are also coming to realize the value of such aid. Although some firms specify that courses
must be job related, others take the view that any additional education increases the effectiveness of the employee. Amounts of aid
vary from 50 to 100 percent of your tuition and fees; occasionally,
the amount depends on your grade in the course. As a rule, neither
course load nor financial need is an issue. For more information
about your company's plan, see your manager or the personnel
office.

Union benefits may take the form of scholarships, tuition re-
bates, or actual college courses sponsored by the union. Such
courses may be offered in conjunction with a local college and
carry college credit. New York's District 65, a major union in the
area of retailing and distribution, has joined forces with Hofstra
University in Hempstead to offer members a complete program
leading to a B.S. degree in social science, at no charge to the student. Professional organizations in such fields as teaching, law enforcement, and health may also provide educational benefits. Details may be obtained from the appropriate office or from a union
representative at work.

Many programs sponsored by businesses or unions cover not
only the individual employee but everyone in the family. If this
could benefit you, be sure to check it out.

Private Sources of Funding

These are the programs people joke about. If your last name is
Leavenworth, there is a scholarship available at Yale—assuming
you are free to relocate in Connecticut, can attend full time, and
meet Yale's entrance requirements. If you are an American Indian
interested in studying agriculture, Cornell University may have
some money for you. There are scholarships for newsboys, caddies,
cheerleaders, and a hundred other groups. A number of excellent

directories are available, cross-indexing the funds by field, level of study, eligibility, and donor. If you are interested, go to the reference room of the best library available to you and check a recent edition of any of the following:

> *Annual Registry of Grant Support.* Chicago, Illinois, Marquis Academic Media.
> *Chronicle Student Aid Annual.* Moravia, New York, Chronicle Guidance Publications. This publisher also has a separate guide to financing graduate study.
> Feingold, S. Norman, and Feingold, Marie. *Scholarships, Fellowships, and Loans.* Arlington, Mass., Bellman Publishing Company.
> Keesler, Oreon. *Financial Aids for Higher Education.* Dubuque, Iowa, William C. Brown Company.
> Mathies, M. Loraine, ed. *Scholarships, Fellowships, Grants, and Loans.* New York, The Macmillan Company. This is also referred to as the "Blue Book."
> Suchar, Elizabeth W. *The Official College Entrance Examination Board Guide to Financial Aid for Students and Parents.* New York, Monarch Press.

More specialized directories include:

> Millsaps, Daniel. *The National Directory of Grants and Aids to Individuals in the Arts.* Washington, D.C., Washington International Arts Letter.
> Proia, Nicholas C., and DiGaspari, Vincent M. *Barron's Handbook of American College Financial Aid.* Woodbury, New York, Barron's Educational Series. This directory is limited to funding available through colleges. The authors have also prepared a separate volume covering only two-year colleges.

Start with any of the general directories; by and large they cover the same ground. You will probably enjoy browsing; where else could you discover that a special scholarship is available to would-be veterinarians "interested in World of Dogs or who have participated in junior handling classes at dog shows"? Whether you will locate any useful leads is another question. Most private funds are intended for full-time students, often fresh out of high school. Many require an above-average academic record. Others specify the field of study, the state, even the college and department.

The directories are fun, they are well organized, and who knows—you may find the perfect scholarship, tailor-made for you, and sail through your studies without a worry in the world.

RESTRICTED PROGRAMS

Although not everyone is eligible for the programs described in this section, they are designed for large groups of students and carry substantial private or government support.

Veterans' Benefits

If you are a veteran or married to one, you will certainly want to determine whether you qualify for benefits under the G.I. bill. Don't lose any time; studies must begin within ten years of discharge from the service. Maximum payments go to full-time students, but even if you are carrying fewer than six credits, you are usually entitled to tuition and fees. Other programs are also available. For information, contact the office of veterans' affairs on any campus; they'll gladly answer your questions regardless of whether you are applying to their school. Or call your local Veterans Administration office; it's listed in the phone book under U.S. Government. *Federal Benefits for Veterans and Dependents, S-1 Fact Sheet* covers financial aid and a variety of other programs. You can get a free copy by writing to Veterans Administration, Washington, DC 20420.

Some states offer their own programs of veterans' benefits. Check it out on campus or by writing to the appropriate agency listed in Appendix 3.

In addition, veterans and their families are eligible for an impressive number of private scholarships and loans. These are described in the booklet *Need a Lift?*, which you can get by sending fifty cents to The American Legion, Dept. S, Box 1055, Indianapolis, IN 46206.

Programs for Women

As a woman, you're automatically eligible for a growing number of special financial aid programs. Some are open to all women, but others specify that the candidate be over twenty-one—or twenty-five, or thirty—mature, or have family responsibilities. For current information, send for the following:

> *Financial Aid: A Partial List of Resources for Women.* Free from the Project on the Status and Education of Women, Association of American Colleges, 1818 R Street, NW, Washington, DC 20009.
>
> *Educational Financial Aid Sources for Women.* Free from Clairol Loving Care Scholarships Program, 345 Park Avenue, New York, NY 10022.
>
> *Educational Financial Aids.* Send $1.00 to American Association of University Women, 2401 Virginia Avenue, NW, Washington, DC 20037.

Many state branches of women's organizations award scholarships; you need not be a member to apply. Write to Scholarship, General Federation of Women's Clubs, 1734 N Street, NW, Washington, DC 20036, specifying the state in which you are interested. Your letter will be forwarded to the appropriate office. And don't overlook Catalyst, the national organization already mentioned in chapter 8.

Programs for the Handicapped

Most states provide educational benefits to students with physical handicaps. As a rule, the course of study must prepare for a job. Funds may be provided, not only for tuition, books, supplies, and living expenses, but also for special equipment, transportation, tutors, or aides.

Information can be obtained from your state vocational rehabilitation office; the number is in the phone book, under the name of your state. Alternatively, write to your state legislators, outlining your circumstances; they may provide more extensive information than you could obtain on your own. Visually handicapped students can contact a local agency for the blind. Above all, don't hesitate to apply. Even if you have adjusted to your handicap, you may still be eligible for special funding.

Programs for Minorities

During the last decade, minority groups have increasingly made their presence felt on campus. Certainly, a contributing factor has been the availability of financial aid. If you are a member of a minority group, you can obtain further information by writing to one or more of the following agencies:

Aspira of America
Educational Opportunity Center
205 Lexington Avenue
New York, NY 10016
(for Hispanic students)

Bureau of Indian Affairs
Albuquerque Area Office
Division of Education
P.O. Box 8327
Albuquerque, NM 87198

Chicano Federation of San Diego
County, Inc.
1960 National Avenue
San Diego, CA 92113

League of United Latin-
American Citizens
National Educational Service
Center

400 First Street, NW, Suite 716
Washington, DC 20001

National Association for the
Advancement of Colored
People
1790 Broadway
New York, NY 10019

National Urban League
500 East 62nd Street
New York, NY 10021

United Scholarship Service,
Inc.
Capitol Hill Station
P.O. Box 18285
941 East 17th Avenue
Denver, CO 80218

Other programs may be available through your college. Make sure the financial aid office is aware of your minority status.

Programs for Low-Income Households

If you are unemployed, or if you are a parent in a low-income household, federal or state funds may be available while you pursue job-related studies.

Under certain circumstances, you may attend college while receiving unemployment benefits. Check with your state unemployment insurance office.

The Work Incentive Program (WIN) is designed for unemployed mothers in low-income households. It provides tuition and a modest stipend for expenses. For additional information, contact your state department of social services, state department of labor, or social service worker. Aid to Families with Dependent Children (AFDC) may also be a source of funds.

Two federal programs, the Educational Opportunity Center (EOC) and Talent Search, provide counseling and information on financial aid, tutoring, and other aspects of college attendance. Located in low-income areas, they are designed to serve the residents of the community. EOC is available to anyone in the area. However, Talent Search concentrates on capable and strongly motivated young students; except for veterans, the upper age limit is twenty-seven. To determine the location of the nearest program, write to Information Systems and Program Support Branch, BHCE/DSSVP, Room 3514, ROB-3, U.S. Dept. of Education, 400 Maryland Avenue, SW, Washington, DC 20202.

Programs in Health-Related Fields

If you are interested in nursing or other health-related professions, funds may be available from a variety of federal sources.

The Nursing Scholarship Program provides funds for half- or full-time study leading to a degree; in the past it has assisted close to 10,000 students a year. The program is administered by the individual college. For information and application forms, see your financial aid office or write to Health Resources Administration, Bureau of Manpower Training Support, Room G-23, 3700 East West Highway, Hyattsville, MD 20782.

This agency also provides education loans of up to $2,500 a year or $10,000 altogether in nursing and other health-related fields. Repayment, at an interest rate of only 3 percent, does not begin until nine months after graduation, and under certain circumstances the federal government will absorb most of the loan. For further information contact your financial aid office or write to the above address.

The National Health Service Corps Scholarship Program covers nursing (both undergraduate and graduate), allopathic and osteopathic medicine, dentistry, and public health nutrition (graduate students only). The awards cover tuition, fees, and a stipend of about $500 a month. On graduation, recipients are required to serve in a federally designated health manpower shortage area for a minimum of two years. Criteria for the funds include professional

background and long-term career plans; financial need is not a factor. For further information, call the toll-free number 800-638-
0824.

The Health Education Assistance Loan Program (HEAL) provides loans of up to $10,000 a year for the study of medicine and
other health-related subjects. Applicants must be full-time students
and may not simultaneously receive other federal loans. Details can
be obtained from your college's financial aid office or by writing to
HEAL, P.O. Box 23033, L'Enfant Plaza, Washington, DC 20024.

Law Enforcement Programs

The Law Enforcement Education Program (LEEP) offers loans and
grants to students in areas related to law enforcement. For further
information check with your college's financial aid office or write
to Office of Criminal Justice Education and Training, Law Enforcement Assistance Administration, U.S. Department of Justice,
Washington, DC 20531.

Other Programs

Many corporations have scholarship programs for employees and
their families. For information, see the personnel office. In some
cases, funds may be available through your religious group; check
at your own place of worship. And the old-fashioned athletic scholarship is still around, for women as well as men. Don't wait to be
discovered; recruiters usually concentrate on high school students.
If you think you qualify, identify a few colleges that are strong in
your field and write to the athletic director.

COMPUTERIZED SEARCHES

If the whole question of financial aid is beginning to overwhelm
you, you might try one of the commercial firms that specialize in
locating funds by computer. For a charge of between $50 and $75,
you are provided with a detailed questionnaire; after you fill it out,
the company searches its computer files to locate suitable scholarships and loans.

The effectiveness of this operation depends on how complete

the computer files are and on how well the computer matches funding sources to your particular qualifications and needs. In any case, it may not be suitable for you. You may be directed to scholarships and loans that require you to be a full-time undergraduate and willing to relocate. Some of the most attractive funding programs are open only to entering freshmen. And of course, the company furnishes only information; there is no guarantee that you will actually receive any financial aid.

If, with all these caveats, you are still interested, contact the firm—without sending any money!—as soon as possible, preferably a year or more before you plan to return to school. At the same time try to locate a few people who have used the service, and find out if they were satisfied. (Don't depend on references furnished by the company; they may not be typical.) When materials arrive, examine them carefully. In particular, see whether the firm guarantees to provide a minimum number of leads, and whether they will arrive in time to be of any use. Bear in mind that *"up to* twenty-five sources" is not the same as "twenty-five sources." Then, if you are willing to take a chance, give it a try. Let us know how it works out.

One last caution. Individual financial aid advisers vary. Even the best of them have their off days. If you feel that potential sources of funding are being overlooked, find a tactful way to point it out. If necessary, arrange to speak with some other member of the staff, or double-check their efforts by doing some research of your own. Financial aid may be the key to your whole reentry program. Don't let it slip away.

Ten

Coping: The Academic Side

You've made it.

You've applied and been accepted, you've gone through the registration procedure, you've filled out everything in triplicate, you've persuaded the gym department that at thirty-one you don't need permission from "parent or legal guardian" to take swimming, you've bought new notebooks with the college seal on the cover—you're in.

Now you are face to face with the real business of college: learning. And it has you worried.

It needn't. Patricia Cross, reporting on a previous study by Roelfs, notes that:

> Older students . . . are more likely to know what they want out of college, to be challenged rather than bored by their classes, to feel self-confident about their ability to keep up with their studies and to understand what is being taught, to spend more time studying, and to express satisfaction with their classes and their instructors.

So put your mind at rest; your chances are just fine. And there are many steps you can take to make them even better, now and after classes get under way. But if there is one key idea, it's this: on the college level, learning is not something that just happens to you; it is something in which you become actively, vigorously involved.

AGGRESSIVE LEARNING

In high school, the student's attitude toward his instructors is likely to be "Teach me." In college, it's "Help me to learn." Learning is something in which you play an active, even an aggressive role. Reading specialist Margaret Waters refers to the "adversary relation" between reader and author. As you read, you reflect, weigh, challenge. You talk back—mentally, if not in fact. The same applies to listening in class.

Perhaps the most important question you can ask yourself is "Why do I need to know this?" In a world with more facts and figures than anyone could possibly remember or digest, why is the instructor concentrating on this particular material?

Sometimes facts must be learned in and of themselves. This includes, say, French vocabulary, English spelling, and occasional formulas from mathematics or science that you need right now, even though their derivation is beyond the scope of the course.

More often, facts are presented as evidence for underlying trends, explanations, or theories that are central to any study of the subject. Details take their place in a mosaic that ultimately reveals a larger pattern. This is why they are included in the first place. The Boston Tea Party is discussed in an American history course, not merely because it is a good story but because historians are interested in the causes of revolutions in general and of the American Revolution in particular. This incident helps us understand the colonists' frame of mind.

Each field of study assembles facts in its own way, for its own purposes. In literature they clarify an author's meaning, his techniques, or the influence of his time on his writing. In science they are used to create and defend theories. History—not only political history, but the history of specific subjects like music and art—draws on facts to establish cause and effect and to identify trends. If you are studying Renaissance art, the fact that Leonardo da Vinci was born in 1452 and Raphael in 1483 indicates that Leonardo might have influenced Raphael—certainly not the other way around. When you learn that Raphael first saw Leonardo's work at the age of twenty-one, and that his paintings thereafter showed a marked change of style, you have the makings of a theory.

The best way to benefit from your courses is to watch for the broad ideas and use them as a framework for the facts. A hundred facts in and of themselves are all but impossible to keep track of; a hundred facts organized around three or four underlying principles begin to make sense. If you have trouble identifying the principles, speak to your instructor. Explain that although you can cope with each day's work, you do not see how it is adding up. Let the instructor take it from there.

Once you perceive what your instructors are driving at, decide for yourself whether they are really making their points. Test out each new piece of information. See where it fits; see *whether* it fits. If you find the evidence unimpressive, don't hesitate to say so.

This, of course, requires that you keep up with your work. Completing each assignment on schedule will provide the facts you need to make your points. Attending class regularly eliminates the risk that you are raising questions which were answered the day you were out. Sitting up front will help you get involved; psychologically, as well as physically, it brings you closer to the action.

Don't be afraid to speak up. Perhaps the instructor will bring in new information to strengthen his case. Perhaps there are decisive arguments that you really cannot appreciate just yet. On the other hand, you may be expressing a recognized alternative point of view. Faculty members usually accept informed disagreement, even from novices. It is disagreement without benefit of insight or facts that irritates them.

The emphasis on ideas is one of the chief distinctions between high school and college. In college facts are only a starting point. It's your business to digest, analyze, and interpet them, and to hammer out your own position. That is what it means to learn aggressively. Success depends not only on what you read or hear but on how profoundly you become involved with it.

We've put active learning first because it is a key to achievement in every course. But there are a host of other ways in which you can help yourself.

BUILDING A GOOD FOUNDATION

Make life easier, not harder. Does this seem obvious? Look at some of your classmates.

Josh signed up for a German class that overlapped the last hour of his physics lab. He decided he could complete the labs quickly and get to German on time. He was wrong. Not only did he mess up his physics course but he squeaked through German with a D.

Adrienne saw college not merely as the start of school but as the start of a new way of life. She would carry twelve credits (on top of her job!), go on a diet, overhaul her wardrobe, and learn to drive—all at the same time. The diet went first. Then the driving; she gave up when she started getting bills for canceled lessons. That's when she decided the old wardrobe would serve a few more months, dropped one of her courses, and completed the rest creditably. The next semester she earned eight credits and managed to lose five pounds. The following summer she learned to drive.

If you have a choice between Professor Smith's section of required geology and Professor Jones's, don't choose Professor Jones's merely because "she really makes you work." She certainly does; perhaps that's why 43 percent of last semester's class either withdrew or failed. Choose Professor Jones's section if geology is important to you, if you already know something about the field, or if you honestly want to learn as much geology in one semester as you conceivably can. Don't choose it merely because it's a challenge. College will be amply challenging without your making it more so.

Don't overload. We have said it before: Whether you are in a traditional or an off-campus program, start with less rather than more.

Sandra, returning to college after nine years of work and family responsibilities, saw herself as only a "fair" student. Her first semester, she took one course—beginning Spanish. She handled it so well that the next term she added Spanish literature in translation and, for a change of pace, a dance class. By the end of the year, convinced that studying and learning were within her grasp, she branched out into psychology, history of the American Indian, and a continuation of Spanish. At the rate of three courses a semester, she completed her A.A. in four years and is now a psychology major at a four-year college.

Overloading is often the result of financial aid programs that require you to be a full-time student. If tuition is not too expensive, ask yourself whether you wouldn't be better off carrying fewer courses, even if it means paying your own way. If you must carry a full load, plan a balanced program to get the most out of each course. We'll return to this subject later in the chapter.

Review and update your background. This is something you can do long before the first day of class.

Only a returning student knows the paralysis that can set in at the sound of such terms as *logarithms, irregular verbs,* or the *Mexican-American War.* Even if the instructor is prepared to review the material, you are in a state of panic—and working your way out of it may take quite a while. So if you are taking a subject with which you have had previous contact, review what you know and, if necessary, bring it up to date. This is true even if the new course does not specify earlier ones as prerequisites. In science, updating may be critical; the theories you learned only a few years ago can already be obsolete. Review is also important in mathematics, history, and foreign languages, where details play a large part.

You don't need college-level texts for this brushup; a paperback review book or high school text can serve very well. But allow plenty of time. The process usually starts with instantaneous terror, which must abate before you can actually buckle down to the job at hand.

For guidance in reviewing or updating your background, ask one or two faculty members who have taught the course you are about to begin. They'll be so impressed with your interest that if you're not actually in their classes, they'll wish you were.

Learn about the library. Libraries are undergoing a revolution. You can learn about them even before the semester begins, certainly before your first library assignment.

Obviously, there are books—thousands upon thousands. They are usually arranged by either the Dewey decimal or The Library of Congress system, although some schools have set up systems of their own. Find out how it is done at your college.

What isn't on hand can often be borrowed for you. Today, libraries by the hundreds have formed vast networks to "pool" their collections. A computer hookup enables each of them to check a title and ascertain in a minute or less where in the network it can be found. If you want a book that is not in your own library, the librarian can often have it in your hands within forty-eight hours.

Computers can also be used to provide you with lists of books and articles on whatever subject you have in mind. It can search under several headings; for example, if you are interested in the housing problems of Hispanics, you can instruct the computer to provide only those references that use both *housing* and *Hispanics* as key words. There is usually a charge for the service, and it may take up to a week, but it can save you hours of tedious research.

There are more directories and guides than you have ever dreamed of. There are directories of organizations, abbreviations, businesses, book reviews, films, psychological tests, and mathematical symbols. There are directories of famous scientists, writers, women, blacks, and professors—yes, you can look up the members of your faculty, if they qualify. And of course, there is a directory of directories.

But books are only part of what you will find. There may be collections of maps and illustrations. Even a small library will have records, films, and videotapes, along with the playback equipment. Extensive collections on microfilm or microfiche save precious funds and even more precious space; the equivalent of thousands of volumes can be stored in a single cabinet. Using this material requires special viewers, but some libraries have small-scale models that you can borrow for use at home.

The more you know about these resources, the easier your library work will be. See whether your library has an explanatory pamphlet or conducts tours. Otherwise, the way to learn is to ask. Get to know the librarians by sight and by name; say hello when you come in. Ask for help occasionally even if you think you can manage on your own; you can be sure they will suggest resources you never would have found independently. But watch whom you ask. A part-time aide, however cooperative, may know less than you do.

Try using the library just for fun. It has hundreds of readable novels, children's books, magazines, and even best sellers. If you are pressed for time, the college library can often save you a trip to the one in town.

Finally, if you are getting frantic because every book you need is on reserve, try joining forces with friends at other colleges. The materials you need may circulate freely over there, and vice versa.

Basic skills. Almost every college offers courses to improve your basic skills in reading, writing, and math. If you can benefit from such a course, think of it as the best thing that ever happened to you. Not only will you need the skill for the rest of your life but you may never have another chance to learn it, or to learn it so well.

Today's remedial courses are among the most innovative and effective educational programs in the country. Step into a modern reading lab and you may not recognize that you are in school at all. A *reading pacer* displays lines of text at a faster or slower rate, depending on the reader's ability. Filmstrips and audiotape are used simultaneously, so that you learn to pronounce each word as you master its meaning. Special equipment enables experts to monitor the eye movements of weak readers. You are provided with a wealth of individualized practice material while aides stand by to provide one-to-one tutoring. In addition, reading courses may include study skills and the use of the library.

In math the entire remedial program may be offered in a self-paced, no-penalty format. You learn at your own rate, take tests as you feel ready for them, and retest on the same material until you attain a passing grade (usually at least 75 percent; 60 percent is seldom good enough in math). All courses may be available on videotape, while practice takes place at a computer that gently corrects your mistakes. Individual tutoring is found everywhere, and some colleges even maintain a twenty-four-hour "hot line" so you can phone in your questions and have them answered at any hour of day or night. On top of this, the anxiety-alleviation programs of many mathematics departments will vastly improve your outlook and self-confidence.

Writing remediation is slower and more painstaking. Some students panic at the very idea of putting words on paper. Others have never been taught the fundamentals of spelling or grammar. A number fill the page with sentences that, although technically correct, have not very much to say. Compounding these problems is the fact that writing is used in so many different ways: to describe, to persuade, to tell a story, to express yourself, and to teach or explain. Faced with these demands, faculty members advance first on one front and then on another. Videotapes and computers are sometimes used, but they are no substitute for individually read, carefully corrected papers.

Writing programs rarely end with remediation. Virtually all colleges have freshman composition courses, required of all students. Many schools provide a "walk-in writing laboratory" where students at any level, with or without appointments, can come for help.

Even if you are not assigned to basic skills courses, look into them if you think they can help. Find out whether learning labs and tutoring services are available to anyone in the college. Alternatively, ask about "transitional" courses, which combine basic skills with college-level work. Whatever your field, from engineering to ballet, the day will come when you will wish you were stronger in basic skills areas. Catch up while you have the chance.

THE THEORY AND PRACTICE OF STUDYING

Of course you know how to study. You find a quiet, well-ventilated corner you can call your own. You publicize your work schedule, so that not even your preschoolers will disturb you unless they're in dire distress. You work at each subject for a suitable length of time—long enough for the important ideas to sink in, not so long that the words stop making sense. At exam time you need only a quick review and a good night's sleep, and you find time for both. You know all about it; you have even explained it to other people.

The problem is doing it yourself.

You would love to start work at eight each evening, but the baby insists on whimpering until quarter of nine. Maybe you are a spineless coward, but you find it hard to study through the baby's whimpering.

You adore your cozy corner at home, but you spent the last hour in the library, waiting for a reserved book to be returned so you could get it. You could have revised your anthropology paper in that hour, but unfortunately, it's in the cozy corner back home.

For that matter, it's seven-thirty, you're putting yourself in the right frame of mind for study, and you get a call from your oldest friend, the one you have not seen for months. He is at the airport with three hours between planes, and can you met him for dinner? You can. You do.

We are not advising you to bypass your course work for any or all of these reasons. But neither can you ignore them. They are part of your life. Beware of systems that do violence to the person you are, no matter how good they look on paper. Evolve one around your own preferences, crotchets, methods, or lack of them.

Making time. You never had a spare minute even before returning to school. How can you possibly fit in ten hours a week of study?

In two ways. By making better use of your free time and by giving up some of the things you've been doing.

Start by earmarking specific hours for study, in school and at home. You need both; library work must be done on campus, reports must be typed at home. Which hours? Maybe the one preempted by that TV comedy that's running out of steam. If you are an early bird, the hour each morning when everyone else is still asleep. Your spouse's bowling night or the afternoon when Junior is at Cub Scouts provide hours when you can concentrate on studying without feeling you are shortchanging anyone.

If you are part of a baby-sitting pool, try "pooling" the children in the afternoons. If one child distracts you, two or three won't make it any worse. In return, you'll have your own period of peace and quiet later in the week.

Setting aside specific times for study gets you into the habit of bracing yourself for work. It also alerts the rest of your household that, barring emergencies, you are off limits at those times. But don't reproach yourself if the system doesn't run like clockwork; even a clock runs down now and then.

Apart from these designated time slots, you will find yourself studying at a hundred odd hours. During meals. On the bus. During intermissions at plays. In the office, when everyone else is at a meeting and you haven't much to do. In the playground. While waiting for the dentist, train, bank teller, laundry, hairdresser—one expert estimates that Americans spend up to five years of their lives just waiting! If you drive a lot, look into study cassettes you can use in your car; the librarian can help you here. Or make review tapes of your own to play as you drive. Just don't make impossible demands on yourself. The cafeteria line may be a good place to read a snippet of Jane Austen, but don't expect to stand there unraveling the fine points of Immanuel Kant.

Get into the habit of keeping some study materials on hand at all times, even if it's only a novel or some chemistry formulas written out on index cards. Small snatches of time may be perfect for studying grammar and vocabulary or for solving routine math problems. Some people can make preliminary notes for papers almost anywhere; others find it easy to revise on the run.

Learn the trick of busy people the world over: Use one kind of work as relaxation from another. Ironing or mowing the lawn allows time to reflect on social studies; poetry can be a respite from physics.

But odd moments add up to so much and no more. To free larger blocks of time, you must review how you actually use them and start weeding out.

If it's something you love, don't give it up. Jogging, baking, movies, browsing in department stores—if it soothes your spirits, elevates your mind, or makes you laugh, keep doing it without apologies or regrets. It's the second-string activities you will want to reconsider. Add up the time you spend on the phone with people you saw at lunch and will see again tomorrow. Decide if it is really worth a half-hour to save seventy cents on a pair of gloves you did not exactly need in the first place. If your favorite TV comedy is on from seven to eight, fine; but sitting through the next two shows is sheer inertia.

Should you actually draw up an hour-by-hour schedule? Probably not. If you are systematic by nature, chances are you are already adhering to such a schedule, even without realizing it. And if you are the reverse, you will not only hate your schedule, but you will hate yourself for abandoning it. The important thing is to get the work done, one way or another, not to divide your days like a checkerboard and fill each square.

Where do you study? Everywhere, obviously. But you still need a base of operations at home, if not actually to work at, then to store your papers and books. The more disorganized you are, the more you need it, if only to contain the chaos. If you leave six piles of papers this way and that, in a system known only to you, then they had better be in the exact same place when you come back tomorrow.

Incidentally, if the sight of all those papers makes your blood run cold, one remedy is to use different colors for different purposes. Pink for Spanish, yellow for math, and blue for literature. Or save buff for your first drafts, green for the second, and white for good copy. It organizes your work and cheers you up at the same time.

How do you study? Vigorously. Study is not a spectator sport. It takes muscle—yours. Your raw materials are the words on the page. Your job is to hammer away at them until you extract a hierarchy of facts, ideas, and theories. Then you backtrack to determine if the theories make sense. It requires concentration.

There are probably as many ways to go about this as there are students doing it. Here are some techniques that have worked for other returning adults.

When the assignment calls for reading, most successful students plan on reading twice. Some start by skimming for main ideas, filling in the details the second time around. Others, equally successful, reverse the process. They start with a close reading, pause to consider the structure and direction of the material, and then reread to make sure they have the right perspective. Outlining the assignment not only helps you keep track of details but also brings out—sometimes quite graphically—what they add up to.

Cassettes have already been mentioned as a way to save time while you drive. They are also invaluable if, like many students, you learn more by listening than by reading. Ask the librarian for help in locating tapes that cover the content of your reading assignments.

Start an assignment the day you get it. This has everything to recommend it. If a topic is more demanding than you had expected, you will have time to work out the rough spots. You will have a chance to discuss them with your instructor. Perhaps most important, you will point your mind in the right direction. Just sleeping on the material may provide new insights by morning.

Work in manageable chunks, depending on the subject matter and your own attention span. You can probably read a Shaw play in one sitting, whereas a half-hour of symbolic logic is your limit. If a subject involves close reasoning or lots of detail, several short sessions are usually more effective than a single long one. You can stare at a math problem for hours and not see your mistakes; only the next day does it hit you that 3 times 2 does not equal 9.

Memorize material by copying it on index cards and reviewing it several times a day. Or try setting it to music—any tune that fits. Hum it on the cafeteria line. Remember "Columbus sailed the ocean blue in fourteen hundred ninety-two?" You never did forget it, did you?

If there's one assignment that makes your heart sink—tackle it first. Your reluctance probably has little to do with the work itself. Perhaps you are afraid of breaking ground in an entirely new area. Or tracking down unfamiliar references. Or writing it out neatly before you hand it in. Putting it off will oppress you; you won't do that assignment, and you won't do anything else very well either. But once you start on it, you'll find that it's not nearly as bad as you thought.

Ask your questions and get them answered. That is what your instructor is there for.

Some questions are easily posed and easily answered. You have done the entire Russian translation, except for a single phrase in the third sentence. You ask about it and get a quick reply. Some questions are more difficult; you are confused about a physics experiment and you don't know why. Some are almost impossible even to ask. You are all fouled up. You are floundering. There's nothing solid anywhere; you feel as if you're walking on balloons. Say so.

If you don't want to monopolize class time, see your instructors during office hours. Make it clear—politely but unequivocally—that you are having a problem with the material and you intend to resolve it. Will they think you are stupid? Your goal is to become smarter. They may be annoyed at first, but once they realize that you are not letting go, it will be in their own interest to work with you as thoroughly and effectively as possible. In the end you will not only learn the material but you will probably win their respect. You needed something and you got it. That is worth doing.

Term papers. At the outset of this chapter we saw how instructors use facts and details to support explanations, theories, and trends. On a modest scale, this is what you are attempting in a term paper. The assignment specifies, "Take a position and justify it." "Raise a question and answer it." Give causes; identify trends. A barrage of conjectures is not a term paper; neither is a string of facts.

Often the most difficult part of the paper is choosing the topic. You want something that captures your imagination, that has some importance, and that is still small-scale enough to be manageable. Here adults have the advantage over their younger classmates; with a much broader range of experiences, they have less trouble finding themes that interest them. One approach to the choice of topic is to look for a link with your major field. Kenneth was studying engineering; his history paper dealt with the construction of Gothic cathedrals. He and his professor both learned a lot.

Some students, including the most thoughtful, are apt to choose topics so monumental they would shatter the experts. Joe wanted to write on European education; his instructor suggested that he limit it to French education, and he ultimately narrowed it down to comparison of French high schools and those of the United States. Shelley, a dedicated feminist, chose women in Shakespeare. There are dozens of them, each more fascinating than the last; she finally settled on "Portia: A Precursor of Modern Woman."

If you are stumped by the choice of topic, check with your instructor—but not until you have done some serious thinking of your own. Otherwise he may toss out some altogether unsuitable suggestion and you will be stuck with it.

Once you have chosen a topic, a good way to get started is to mull it over, jotting down on separate index cards all the thoughts that cross your mind. Don't worry about whether they are wise or foolish; write them down anyway. Browse through an article or book on the subject, making notes, not only of the author's position but of your own reactions. Don't rush the process; ideas surface when you least expect them. After a few days, when you have several dozen cards, arrange them by related ideas. Gradually the broad outlines of your paper will begin to take shape.

If your topic anchors the paper, your facts and arguments flesh it out. Now is the time to start gathering evidence. You may draw on your text, your classroom notes, or outside research. Some historical information may be interesting; who else considered this question, and what positions did they take? If you are defending one point of view, it helps to sketch in the alternatives, if only to show why yours is preferable.

Of course, you are still faced with the mechanics of writing. Here the writing lab may be helpful; qualified tutors will steer you to the correct usage. More complex is the problem of organization. The order in which you introduce and justify your theme, support it, and arrive at a conclusion calls for a certain logic. Proportion is equally important. In a ten-page paper, you would not devote the first seven to preliminaries, squeezing all the facts, theories, and conclusions into the remaining three. Faculty members claim that poor organization and lack of proportion reflect poor thinking. That may be severe, but right or wrong, they are calling the tune.

Examinations. "Exam week," reports educator Martha Maxwell,

> is a stressful period for many college students . . . Men students wear old clothes and appear unkempt and unshaven; women take less care in their dress and appearance. Men students tend to eat less and lose weight; women report weight gains and delayed menstrual periods. Both sexes report sleep loss or problems in sleeping, worry more, are fatigued and nervous, and spend less time socializing.

See? You're not the only one.

Your instructor doesn't like examinations any more than you do. Yet they are the standard method for demonstrating what you have learned. If there is a better way, no one has found it.

If you freeze up at the very idea of tests, see the office of student affairs. They may be conducting workshops in such areas as studying for tests, test anxiety, and test-taking techniques. You will learn to read tests, note what is being asked, and provide answers that are to the point. You will take practice tests to ease your panic. You will even discover that a moderate amount of anxiety is beneficial; it is associated with higher scores.

Everyone knows that you are supposed to get a good night's sleep before a test and arrive prepared for anything. Above all, cramming is reprehensible. Still, one must ask—compared to what? Compared to systematic, thorough day in, day out study, it certainly is. Compared to taking your test without an inkling of what has been going on, it may be a valid survival technique. In truth, thousands of students have gone through the experience of studying all night, taking a shower, bracing themselves with coffee and chocolate bars—and passing the final one way or another. We don't recommend it, but it could be better than the alternatives.

A few pointers will help you get through any test.

> Come equipped with what you will need: pens, pencils, calculator, tissues, candy bars, or cigarettes, if they help. If you are having an open-book test, bring the book.
> If your head is crammed with rules, formulas, or dates, jot them

down on your scrap paper the minute you get your exam—certainly *before* you read the questions and surrender to panic.

Then read the entire test. Surprisingly often, one question will suggest the answer to another. Reading the test will also help you allocate your time.

Begin with the questions you are sure you can answer. Then return to those that gave you difficulty.

Avoid distractions if you can. In particular, don't become alarmed as your classmates start leaving the exam. They may have given up altogether; you're still in there fighting.

Test questions are of two types: essay and objective. *Objective questions* test facts rather than ideas; *essay questions* test both.

Essay questions are like miniature term papers and can be approached in the same way; the big difference is that you cannot research your facts and must have them at your fingertips. Before writing anything at all, take a few minutes to think through your answer. Identify your central theme, review your evidence, prepare a short outline, and start working. Occasionally an instructor allows some latitude in the choice of topic. As part of your studying, keep a few ideas in mind against this possibility.

Objective questions come in a variety of forms. *Short-answer* questions are just that; you fill in a blank with a couple of words. If you are not sure of the answer you can be a little vague, but basically either you know it or you don't.

Multiple-choice questions are something else. Most standardized tests, including CLEP and ACT PEP exams, are of this type, chiefly because they are easily graded. A whole theory of test taking has arisen around multiple-choice tests. It is critical to know if you are penalized for wrong answers. If not, guess on *everything;* do not leave a single question blank. Even if there is a penalty, try to eliminate one or two choices and guess among the remainder; you usually have more to gain than to lose.

One could go on in this vein. Hours have been spent debating whether, in guessing, it is preferable to use the same letter all the time (in which case you are virtually sure to get *some* right), or guess randomly (in which case you could get *everything* right!) Occasionally the wording of one question suggests the answer to another. Some students enjoy this battle of wits and do a lot of research "psyching out" multiple-choice tests. Others feel the time is better spent studying.

STANDARDS AND GRADES

How good is good?

When Elliott started his economics course, he knew nothing at all about the subject. Four backbreaking months later, he could at least recognize key names and definitions. He could follow a discussion in the financial pages of the Sunday paper. His term report proved—to him, anyway—that he could gather information and generate ideas in an entirely new field.

But his classmate Marie came from a family of economists and expected to major in it herself. In plain truth, her report was twice as long as his and four times as thorough. The instructor knew nothing about Elliott's struggles or Marie's background, and it would not have mattered if he had. Marie rated A on her paper; Elliott got C—.

The grading was fair. The difficulty was that Elliott had progressed so far in four months, he did not realize how much further there was to go. It was not that his standards were low; it was that he had no basis for setting standards at all. Marie's paper would have been an eye-opener, but of course he never saw it. He did not know how good is good.

This troubles students from disadvantaged backgrounds or from very small schools. It can be aggravated by sluggish teachers who cut corners on their own standards. It may create real difficulties for external degree students who never have a basis for comparison. The problem goes beyond grades; these students may never have the chance to discover their own potential.

If you are working hard and making progress but still seem to be missing the mark, talk to your instructor or an adviser. Point out that you would like to do better but you don't know how to proceed. Perhaps the two of you can go over one of your own papers. Were some important ideas treated superficially? Were others omitted altogether? Did you emphasize minor points at the expense of important ones? What does it mean for an idea to be important in this field?

A session like this can be invaluable, even after grades are in. For one thing, it can raise your standards in every subsequent course you take. For another, grades can be changed; perhaps the instructor will allow you to submit an extra piece of work.

And this takes us to the subject of grades.

If you are like most students, grades have been hanging over your head since you were six. You have been inspected and classified like a cut of meat. No wonder you panic at the word.

But you are grown up now. You are not bringing your report card home to Mom and Dad. Your spouse will not cut off your allowance if you fall below expectations, and your children will probably love you all the more for it.

Of course you want to do well, for every possible reason. But situations arise. Mel returned to college three years ago, determined that this time he would do it right. But he is taking statistics and third-semester calculus, along with a required course in English literature. On top of that, it's tax season and his part-time accounting job has mushroomed into ten hours a day. Deliberately and regretfully, Mel is sacrificing the literature course. Some other time he will discover the joys of Wordsworth and Blake; right now, all he wants to do is pass. He is aiming, not for 60 percent—that's cutting it too close—but for 65 or 70. Just enough to persuade a professor undecided between D and F that he deserves the D. He has set his priorities and is prepared to live with the result.

Like Mel, you may be forced to put all your energies into some courses at the expense of others. Or you have so much on your mind, you cannot make room for all the physiology you are supposed to know. That's when you decide that B is better than C, and C is better than D or F, but you can live with any of them.

Please do not interpret this as encouragement to complete college in a slipshod style. If you are going on to graduate school, you will certainly need the best grades you can manage. In any case, you want to learn as much as possible under the circumstances. But for returning adults, circumstances may mean anything from a transfer out of town to a household laid low by the mumps. What do you do? You remind yourself that passing with a D is better than failing with an F. For that matter, earning the degree with any grade-point average whatever is a lot better than not earning it at all.

One last word on grades. Many colleges now allow a Credit–No Credit, or CR–NCR option; the grade of NCR does not figure in your average and saves you from an F. CR–NCR may get you out of an occasional predicament, but it is no cure-all. Outsiders examining your record invariably perceive the NCR as a disguised F, while CR is usually taken to mean C or D.

PLANNING YOUR PROGRAM

Planning the right program means more than assembling a few courses that meet at different times. Ideally, your program should be manageable, interesting, and get you where you're going.

A top priority is sequential courses. These are found in every department but are critical in mathematics, science, and foreign languages. A two-year Spanish sequence means four separate courses, taken one after another. Skipping even a single semester can set you back. If your field of study involves such sequences, be sure to fit in the necessary courses, term by term.

Vary your academic diet. Different subjects make different demands on you; after an hour of automotive technology, it can be luxurious to unwind in a music or literature course. Computer courses are notorious for running you ragged; two in the same semester may drive you out of your mind. Look out for an overdose of "heavy" courses like math, economics, and statistics, with a large component of abstract quantitative thinking. On the other hand, too many humanities courses will have you drowning in term papers by the end of the semester.

Once you have identified your courses, you are usually faced with a choice of sections. This is the time for another look at your own learning style.

The basic issue in learning styles is whether you learn better on your own or under regular supervision. However, even within the classroom, there are many distinctions. Educator Alfred Canfield has suggested the following:

> Do you see your classmates as teammates or as competitors?
>
> Do you prefer a fluid, spontaneous organization of course content, or one that is more structured?
>
> Do you enjoy setting and achieving your own goals, or do you look to the instructor for direction?
>
> Do you expect an informal relationship with instructors, or do you see them as authority figures?
>
> Would you rather work on your own? In teams? As a class?
>
> Do you benefit from a disciplined classroom, with a sustained high standard of student performance? Or do you prefer a more relaxed setting?

The best way to answer these questions is to analyze those classes that you really enjoyed and benefited from. What were they like? If you enjoy competition, don't deny it merely because it doesn't make you very proud. Answer in terms of the person you are, not the person you might like to be.

Once you identify your own style, you need an instructor who matches it. One source is the student evaluations now required on hundreds of campuses. These evaluations are usually on file for use by students like yourself (as well as by faculty members, who enjoy reading about one another); ask the librarian where to find them. Depending on the questions asked, you will learn about the instructors' spontaneity or lack of it, their classroom manner, speaking voice, use of the blackboard, assignments and tests, and even their approach to grading. A key question is "Would you take another course with this instructor?" In reading the evaluations, bear in mind that students are extravagantly generous; subconsciously, perhaps, they are hoping the favor will be returned.

After you form a first impression from the evaluations, round it out by speaking to other students. You might even visit a classroom or stand outside the door and watch the professor in action.

If, with all your planning, one or two classes disappoint you, you are permitted to make changes the first week of the semester. However, this is not as straightforward as it sounds. Dropping courses is easy, but the ones you want to substitute may already be full. One way to resolve this problem is to sign up for an extra course or two in the first place. After attending the first few days of class, you will know which courses are likely to work out and which are not. Then you simply drop those that are least satisfactory, and you are left with the course load you intended all along. Tuition is usually refunded for courses dropped this early in the semester, so it will not cost you anything extra.

Eleven

Coping: The Nonacademic Side

Coping. Knowing your way around. Working within the system. These are a far cry from the business of learning, but they can make that business go a lot more smoothly.

GETTING ACCLIMATED

Even before classes start, learn the geography of the campus. Get a map. You may find one in the college bookstore—assuming you can locate the bookstore without a map.

Go through a dry run of your first day's schedule. Arrive on campus by car, bus, however you normally would, and make your way from building to building, classroom to classroom, just as you would if school had begun. If you are attending evening classes, go through the process at that time; things look different at night. Find out how long it takes. Learn which elevators are local and which express, where they stop, and anything else there is to know about them. One student waited all period for a down elevator on the tenth floor, only to discover it stopped only on nine.

Learn where to buy snacks, cigarettes, yellow pads—whatever you need to tide you over. Track down a few washrooms and public phones, along with the nurse's office, cafeteria, and library. Leave a copy of your schedule with the family so they can locate you in case of emergency. All this takes only an hour and will add immeasurably to your assurance.

Buy your textbooks ahead of time. Not only will you have your books before the supply runs out—and at a savings because you will have first crack at used copies!—but you will avoid one of the most spectacular mob scenes this side of Hollywood. If the bookstore does not know which books have been selected, check with the separate departments. If there is a change of text or you drop the course, you usually get a full refund for the books you have bought.

Learn your instructors' names, including spelling and pronunciation. Addressing them by name the first day is a good way to get acquainted. Don't worry about their official titles. If you call them all professor, no one will complain.

These steps should help ease you into the college routine. At that point you can seriously start learning about the system.

GETTING TO KNOW THE ROPES

Any time you have several thousand people in one place, you are going to have problems.

I don't feel good.

Can I borrow records to take home? Even if I'm not taking a music course?

I forgot my books in my professor's office and now it's locked. Can anybody help me?

Everybody tells me a psychology major is worthless without a graduate degree. Where can I talk it over?

I think someone's following me.

I want to study in Europe. Will the courses count here? What will it cost?

I don't know what's the matter with me. I feel like crying all the time.

I missed the midterm because my kid was sick. Can I have a makeup?

I missed the midterm because my kid was sick, and the professor won't give me a makeup!

How do you meet people on this campus?

I lost my wallet and don't have a dime!

I must contact my teacher right now. Why won't you give me his phone number?

She flunked me without even reading my paper!

I need a job.

These are only a fraction of the hundreds of problems that arise on campus every day. Knowing what facilities are available to solve them will make every aspect of college easier for you.

Dropping Courses

If you ever learned to drive, you will remember that the first step was how to start the car. The second was how to stop it.

Just as there are procedures for getting into a course, so there are procedures for getting out of it. You do not just stop attending. That, on most campuses, rates you a grade of Unofficial Withdrawal, equivalent to an F. If you drop a course early enough, you may be able to substitute another. (With the instructor's permission, you can often do this even beyond the official change of program period.) Or you may be eligible for a complete or partial tuition refund. If you drop it later in the semester, an interview with an adviser may be recommended. In any case, check the catalog under "Withdrawals" and familiarize yourself with the procedure. You needn't learn the details; you may never need them. What *is* important is knowing the procedure exists.

Extracurricular Activities

Whatever your interest, the campus will have a club, committee, or special-interest group devoted to it. They are serious and they should be taken seriously. In many communities college concerts and plays are among the best in town. The newspaper is independent and stimulating; by comparison, the private local papers seem to contain nothing but supermarket ads, obituaries, and miscellaneous trivia. Special-interest groups propagandize and lobby for political issues of immediate concern, like financial aid and improved facilities. Not only are they vigorous and effective but they've learned to combine these traits with a certain amount of courtesy and tact.

Extracurricular activities can take an unlimited amount of time—and may be worth it. They provide a channel for expressing and acting on your convictions. Key student positions—the editorship of the paper or a high office in the self-government association—can earn you college credit, as a form of independent study. There may even be a cash stipend of several hundred dollars a semester, although when you stop to figure it out, you will find you have been working for twenty cents an hour. More important, these positions often serve as entering wedges in professions that would otherwise be murderous to crack.

Even if you do no more than look in on an occasional meeting, extracurricular activities are a wonderful way to make friends. Everyone is there voluntarily and everyone shares a common interest. As a returning adult you will have a chance to bridge the generation gap and get acquainted with younger classmates. You'll marvel at the maturity of these students—especially in contrast to yourself at their age! And you all have enough in common to make the differences stimulating.

Student Services

Until the 1970s student services were skimpy and routine. Then, under the impetus of student demands, they expanded in all directions until today they touch on every aspect of student life. Read the full description in the catalog; it can be the most valuable half-hour of your college career. Here's a sample.

Career counseling and placement. This office does a lot more than match up students and part-time jobs. Trained counselors will discuss your major and career goals, provide information on job opportunities, and even get on the phone to find entry-point jobs for graduating seniors. They sometimes administer tests of aptitudes and special skills. They run workshops on how to ferret out job openings, prepare a résumé, and make the most of an interview. Their placement services are often available to alumni indefinitely. And all of it is free.

Academic advising goes far beyond telling you which courses you must take. It's the clearinghouse for information on graduate schools, scholarships, and opportunities to study abroad. It administers independent study, CLEP exams, and life experience programs. Academic advising may sponsor sessions on test taking, study skills, and choosing a major. They also follow up student appeals on academic issues, including exemptions and grades.

Counseling services. Here you can find skilled professionals with whom you can talk about anything that's bothering you. Family, sex, grades, drugs—this is the place. Short-term help may be provided right on the premises; more complex problems are referred to an outside agency. Workshops are offered in such areas as assertiveness training, human sexuality, and problems of returning adults. Don't be self-conscious about using the counseling service. Everyone runs into difficulties; the secret is to deal with them while they are still small enough to be manageable.

The ombudsman, while not under the direct supervision of student services, usually has ties to them. He—or she—is simply a respected, seasoned individual responsible for investigating complaints and grievances by any member of the college community. If you feel you have been unfairly treated, the ombudsman will advise you of appeals procedures, recommend appropriate corrective action, and even suggest that college procedures be changed to eliminate a recurrence of the problem. When possible, your anonymity will be respected if you request it. Usually the ombudsman has only moral force, not specific official authority. However, his standing in the college is so high that his mere intervention has a power of its own.

Do not conclude from this that your problems cannot possibly be important enough for the ombudsman. That's why he's there. Don't nurture your grievances; you are much better off bringing them into the open.

Student services also operates the financial aid office and provides advisers to veterans, foreign students, adults, and other special groups. In a crisis they can lend you a few dollars, find you a place to sleep, or put you in touch with a legal agency. Their staff includes some of the nicest people on campus. If you have a problem, large or small, a question that has not been answered, if you feel you have been getting the runaround, this is the place to go.

GETTING WHAT YOU NEED

As a student, you are protected by procedures you may not even know about. At most schools, your rights include all of the following.

You have the right to appeal a grade, usually through the office of academic affairs. There is no such thing as a final grade; grades can be changed long after the end of the semester.

You have the right to review your final examination with the instructor. You will see where you lost credit and have a chance to ask questions about it.

You have the right to meet with your instructor during office hours. If the instructor isn't there, call it to the attention of the department chairman. The responsibility for providing office hours is taken seriously at most colleges.

You have the right to see the department chairman if you feel the instructor's approach is detrimental to the class. If essential topics are being skipped, if substantial amounts of class time are used for other than class business, if there appears to be a bias against women or minorities, if the instructor is absent or has a habit of coming late—speak up. However, because problems like these affect the entire class rather than you alone, it's appropriate for the class to come as a group.

You have the right to miss tests, including the final, for illness or personal emergency. Every semester, between 3 and 5 percent of all students miss final examinations for legitimate reasons. The college has procedures for makeup tests; the professor knows all about them. You are *entitled* to stay home.

You have the right not to bear the brunt of other people's mistakes. If a test or report gets lost, it's the instructor's problem, not yours. For all kinds of reasons you may choose to do it over, but it is not an obligation.

This is only a sampling of your rights. Some are tacitly understood by the administration, while others are spelled out in the college catalog or charter. Read them; they may surprise you.

But in addition, you have the right to ask for anything that you want. Your instructor in turn has the right to refuse your request. Or grant it.

Barbara felt that her physics final did not represent her best work. She requested an extra assignment to raise her grade, pointing out that whether she succeeded or not, she would certainly learn some more physics. The instructor mapped out a project that ultimately changed her C to a B.

Paul felt he could learn more history if he worked on his own. He and his instructor worked out an arrangement in which he reported only for tests and an occasional conference. It hurt no one and it helped Paul.

Sadie had to have a morning program because her baby-sitter left at noon. She implored the biology instructor to admit her to a closed section—and got in. Sadie had no way of knowing it, but the instructor herself was faced with the same problem.

Claude needed another three weeks for his term paper. He was candid; he had underestimated the complexity of the subject and needed more time to do it justice. Permission was granted.

If, for suitable reasons, you feel that a particular rule should be waived in your case, request it. Do not shrink into yourself murmuring that you don't want to be an exception. You *do* want to be an exception, and you probably deserve it. Administrators rarely discuss the fact, but rules are waived all the time. There is nothing unfair about it except, perhaps, that hundreds of equally deserving students do not have the assurance to follow your example.

Meet the College Halfway

You have come to see the librarian, and a half-hour later she is still on her coffee break. You are steaming! So that's where your tuition goes! Who does she think she is?

On the other hand, you could use the time to complete another assignment. She'll be back by the time you're done. Maybe it was not a coffee break at all, but a delayed lunch hour.

College regulations allow smoking if it's done in a single area near the back of the room. Professor Black requests that there be no smoking at all. Clearly, you are right; he is wrong. But you are in that room only fifty minutes, whereas he is there all day. Perhaps there are health factors you don't know about. And whatever improves the professor's functioning will surely help students as well. You can give up smoking for three periods a week.

Coping may be no more than striking the right balance between adapting to the college and having the college adapt to you. We do not recommend backing away from a fight—if the issue is important and you believe you are right. But it takes time, involvement, and energy. Try yielding on the small issues so you can hold your ground on the big ones.

Living with Red Tape

You have come to the physics department for evaluation of a course taken elsewhere. The adviser is sitting there, doing nothing at all, as far as you can see. Can you go up and talk to him? You cannot. You complete a form.

You are at the registrar's, dropping Elementary Latin, and you have been asked to fill out seven identical cards by hand. In an era of computers, copying machines, and men on the moon, you are filling out seven cards by hand. In a course where nobody even knows you are there.

It is already March, and last term's Incomplete in Statistics still has not been changed to the C you ultimately earned. You have been leaving notes for the professor, but apparently he has been at a conference in Istanbul. No one else has the authority to do it. If the grade is not changed by June, it turns to F.

Red tape exists everywhere, but the red tape in colleges is redder, stickier, and there's more of it. If businesses were run this way, they would be down the drain in a month!

There is truth in the charge, but there are several explanations.

For one thing, the stock-in-trade of registrars is far more precious than that of the average business. If the dry cleaner loses your jacket, the matter can be resolved for a few dollars. If the registrar loses your credits, he or she has lost something unique and irreplaceable. (Imagine if, by way of compensation, you were offered a tuition refund!) Students' rights require the documentation of every credit. The college's reputation depends on giving credit only where credit is due. Hence a meticulous record-keeping system is needed, with every entry checked and double-checked. Seven cards.

Admittedly, this could be better done by computer. But colleges do not have the cash flow of businesses. Computerization is still getting there. The school teaches computer science, but its own programming is a patchwork, created by part-time employees who went on to better jobs in industry. As for copying machines, any department chairman will tell you the two-cents-a-copy charges really add up.

But with all these problems out of the way, the wheels of college administration would still turn slowly. Some of the difficulty can be traced to the faculty. Perhaps appropriately, their priorities lean toward research, writing, and teaching; routine paperwork ranks low. The letter you send today may not be answered for a month or more. On top of this, the faculty may spend surprisingly little time on campus, as you have discovered if you have ever tried to track them down. They go away, sometimes for weeks. When a businessman leaves town, someone else takes over his correspondence. But college faculty members are autonomous. When Professor X goes to Istanbul, the letters pile up until his return.

We are describing the situation, not defending it. It could improve, particularly if a little pressure were applied. But colleges will probably continue to move slowly for years to come.

Where does that leave you? Resigned. You can raise your voice, tear up the cards, and send a letter to the editor, but you will end up in the same place. Relax; at least you have more patience than you did as a teen-ager. Live with it.

By the way, did you want to know what happens to all those cards? One each to the Latin department and the instructor. One to the financial aid office, in case dropping Latin puts you below the minimum course load. One to the office of institutional research, for their statistical studies of things like dropping courses. One to the office of student affairs, where everyone's program is on file. One to the registrar. And the last one to you, so you know what's going on in your life.

GETTING ALONG

Starting college can unsettle your personal relations. The organization of colleges is almost military, from president to lowly adjunct instructor, from Ph.D. candidate to freshman. You have no sense, as yet, of where you fit. Meanwhile, there is a subtle change in your relation to family, to friends, and to yourself. Things need to be worked out.

Finding Your Place on Campus

College has been described as a great leveler, where each person is accepted on the same terms: student. One of the great opportunities will be to reacquaint yourself with the eighteen-to-twenty-two-year age group. The age gap will close as you immerse your-selves in the common problems of checking assignments, studying, or reviewing for a test.

In each class you will gradually identify one or two "buddies." You will fall back on each other in case of absence or utter confusion; you will exchange notes, study together for tests, and provide mutual encouragement and support. Some of these buddies may be little older than your children. The relationship will not necessarily demand intimacy, but it will be warm and comfortable.

For closer friendships, you are more likely to seek out your own contemporaries, if only because they are faced with the same problems. Fortunately, the adult student is no longer a novelty. In today's community colleges, the average age is twenty-six and going up: certainly you will not feel isolated.

Your relations with instructors are on a different level. From the academic point of view there is no problem; most instructors are delighted to work with adult students. Often the "drop-ins" have such zest and enthusiasm for what they are learning that they invigorate the entire classroom. In response, the professor strips away the busywork and makes learning more direct and satisfying.

What may unnerve you is the initial realization that the kid in sneakers and Levis is your economics professor. You remember professors as *old*—graying, respectable, walking with slow steps. Gradually, you come to terms with the fact that they are your age or even younger.

This has its advantages. Many junior faculty members are themselves in graduate school and know what you are going through. Women instructors may be working mothers, using the same child-care center that you do. If your burden of work, family, and school threaten to get the better of you, you can count on their sympathy and support.

This does not mean you are friends. Even if your instructors are exactly your age, live in the same neighborhood, and shop at the same supermarket, they're the instructors and you the student. As long as they're giving the grades and you are getting them, it is hardly a two-way relationship. Later on, the instructors you see at the child-care center or tennis clinic may become your friends, but at least until the end of the semester, it's more comfortable to keep things on a relatively formal footing.

Dropping Back In and Your Family

You can be at odds with your family for a day. A week. But you will be going to college for years. You have no choice but to enlist their support.

Typically, adult students report that both spouses and children are generous in their cooperation and encouragement. But don't stretch your luck. Back up their inherent goodwill with some careful planning of your own.

Dropping back in and the children. School-age children are usually delighted to see their parents returning to school. The very idea of Mom or Dad struggling with homework, cramming for tests, and bringing home the grown-up equivalent of a report card is instantly and irresistibly hilarious. And be assured that if you should fail a course or squeak through with a D, you'll have all their sympathy and understanding.

On the plus side, children often take their own studies more seriously when they observe the importance you attach to yours. They are more willing to talk over their problems—not just the nuts and bolts of daily assignments, but the pressures they may be experiencing. For your part, your own agonies with Russian or tax law may open your eyes to your children's difficulties. "I never had any trouble in grade school," one parent notes, "so I pooh-poohed my kid's gripes about spelling and math. Now that I'm going nuts getting my computer programs to run, I know how he feels!"

Preschoolers, too, can be helped to adapt to their new lifestyle. Studies have shown that toddlers thrive in suitable day-care facilities. Far from being hurt by the arrangement, they become more peer-oriented and self-sufficient and show few adverse effects.

We are talking averages. If you own child appears to be having difficulties, give it a little time, talk to the staff, and then, if the situation persists, look for alternatives.

The one inescapable problem with child-care arrangements outside your own home is that they fall apart when the child becomes ill. You simply cannot bring Jenny to her day-care center when she's suffering from tonsillitis, earache, or upset stomach— and it is a rare child that makes it through the year without one or another of these ailments.

What to do? Try calling on a cooperative friend or relative, a housekeeper, or a baby-sitter with whom you have established a working relation. Once in a very long while, your school pressures may be so great that your spouse will stay home from work while you attend class. Otherwise—you stay home yourself. You get the assignments from friends in your courses and keep up as best you can. If it's one of those years when the family comes down with one ailment after another, talk to your instructors and the office of student services. Drop some of your courses if necessary; salvage the remainder. Consider preparing at home for CLEP exams. Next year the household may be flourishing, and you can pick up where you left off.

Dropping back in and your spouse. One thing you may be sure of: your return to college will have endless repercussions on your spouse. These effects may be justified in the long run but for the present, even in the smoothest marriages, they are real deprivations. Husbands complain that their wives bypass movies, sex, and routine domestic chores for the sake of their studies. Wives, already involved with young children all day, find that they are now involved evenings as well. If emotions are tinged by insecurity, misgivings, a sense of guilt or inadequacy, the problems can run very deep.

For returning women, the difficulty is compounded by the fact that while everyone pays lip service to equal rights, today's men and women were themselves raised in households that followed traditional patterns. We learn from our role-models; if you grew up thinking of Dad as the breadwinner and Mom as the great American homemaker, you cannot shake the image overnight. A recent survey of engaged couples found that

> Young people now getting married have highly traditional views of what to expect from a spouse and how they should act themselves . . . Young women automatically assume they will have to take over most of the household tasks regardless of their own careers . . . [Young men] automatically act in a dominant way rather than as an equal partner.

Do not be taken in by glowing newspaper accounts of young couples who share and share alike; the reason they are written up in the first place is that they are very, very rare.

Another difficulty is that dropping back in often gives one

partner a marked educational edge over the other. Lucy, with only a semester of community college behind her, acknowledges that her husband's degree will give the family a tremendous advantage in the long run; but for the present, she is aware only of her acute pain in seeing him outdistance her. The theory of taking turns at dropping back in—"I get my degree, then you get yours"— sounds good, but in practice it can require the better part of a decade.

Friction over your returning to school does not mean that your spouse is unloving, destructive, or undependable, but the adjustment takes time. The following steps may help smooth the path.

Carry fewer courses. Grant your spouse at least the same status as a required math or history course: eight or ten hours a week of undiluted time and attention. If you cannot fit in that much time, carry one course less.

If being away from home is creating problems, ask whether— for the present, at least—independent study may be the answer. The demands of CLEP exams or off-campus projects can be met whenever it suits your family and yourself. Thirty credits earned in this way represent a full year of study toward a degree.

Is it possible for both of you to drop back in? Even if your spouse carries only one course, having the same goals will go a long way toward making the situation livable. You may even find yourselves preparing for the same exams!

Encourage your spouse to join you on campus occasionally, if only for a meal in the college cafeteria. Introduce him or her to faculty and classmates; suggest sitting in on a class or two. Try attending the plays, concerts, lectures, and athletic events sponsored by your college. Stay-at-home spouses often perceive the campus as large, alien, and threatening; familiarity will help overcome fear of the unknown.

Speak with an adviser. This is one problem you undoubtedly share with many of your classmates. Perhaps the college can organize social and cultural events for students and their spouses. Sports facilities can be made available. It may be possible to convert an unused corner of the campus to a lounge with snacks, music, and a few games—a kind of "spouse-care center" where the two of you can meet after class. Anything that involves spouses in campus life will improve conditions for both of you and may even convince them to return to college themselves.

Helping hands. We've been spoiled by those stories of valiant pioneer families where everyone pitches in and the chores are done by noon. Stop deceiving yourself. It does not happen that way anymore. Perhaps it never did.

If you expect your family to help with household chores, start by ascertaining their own preferences. One child may volunteer to water the plants. Another agrees to rake leaves in return for never, never being expected to wash the dishes. Children may willingly prepare dinner if they have a voice in menu planning. After the first spate of overdone hamburgers and spaghetti with catsup sauce, they may actually learn to cook.

Be careful of imposing your own standards on everyone else. Television notwithstanding, families adjust admirably to grayish towels and dust on high shelves. They have an incredible tolerance for built-up grime. When you sit down to discuss chores, spell out not merely who does what, but how often. By their standards, not necessarily yours.

By the same token, don't expect your family to adopt your own high-efficiency cleaning techniques. If you hate housework, you may make a point of getting it done as quickly as possible. Your children's solution may be to enliven it. Junior sprinkles sky-blue scouring powder on the yellow kitchen counter and at once begins to fingerpaint. Susie vacuums the entire living room while talking on the telephone. Billy will wash the bathroom floor only if he can do it barefoot, pretending he's ice-skating. This, too, will pass. Live with it.

Dropping Back In and Your Job

How closely your studies tie in with your job depends on whether you expect to improve your status at your present firm or make a fresh start elsewhere. In the latter case, a low profile may be advisable; your boss may decide that if you are leaving anyway, you may as well leave right now. In this case, think of the "job" in question as the one you'll get *after* graduation. Prepare by taking the right courses, talking to people in the field, and so on.

If you plan to stay where you are, the key step is involving your supervisors in your plans. Let them know what you are doing and ask for further suggestions. Their support is invaluable, not only for financial reasons but because they're in a position to give you time. If the one class you must have is offered only in midafternoon, the right to leave early makes a tremendous difference. If your nontraditional program calls for a week of on-campus residence, your supervisor's cooperation is essential. You may even get that week in addition to your regular vacation time.

To earn these privileges, keep your employers posted on your progress, and particularly on the specific ways in which you are becoming more valuable to the firm. With them in your corner, asking for concessions will be a great deal easier.

Safety Valves

Toward the end of Thornton Wilder's play *The Skin of Our Teeth*, with the world in ruins and the hero searching for the strength to start anew, Sabina, the servant girl, asks if she can go to the movies. The hero is aghast, but she goes on to explain. "Every now and then I've got to go to the movies. I mean my nerves can't stand it."

College is serious and life is more so, but if you push on all fronts all the time, the system is going to collapse sooner or later. One professor, confronted with students who were falling further and further behind, took to asking them what they did for fun. More often than not, they replied, "I don't know . . . nothing, I guess." Despite the fact that they were sacrificing everything for their studies—or perhaps because of it—even their studies were not going well.

No matter how important college may be, don't let the pressures build up. Sabina was right; every now and then you've got to go to the movies. Or the beach. Or partying. Or to a concert or picnic. It's not a self-indulgence; it's the essential oil that keeps the machinery working.

Taking a Break

Earning a degree does not happen overnight. At some point you may feel you are running out of steam.

Luke felt that way when his first child was due. He had been making good progress through a combination of classes and CLEP exams, but his wife seemed tense and was already speculating on how she would ever get out of the house. All signals pointed in the same direction: take a break.

Lauren came to the same decision when she received a promotion to supervisor of the intensive care unit. Her responsibilities were tripled in the new job; she needed time to get her bearings.

Or you may just want a change. If you have not had a proper vacation in years, you have earned the right to pause and relax.

Your first step is to discuss your plans with an adviser. If you are studying on your own, this could require a long-distance telephone call—and be worth it. Don't rack your brain for fanciful excuses. It's enough to say you're saturated and need a break.

In most cases this is no problem at all. Your adviser will probably agree with you, but may at the same time suggest some concrete steps to expedite your return. There will be forms to fill out, and possibly a small fee covering maintenance of matriculation.

You have earned your break; use it however you like. Just circle the date on your calendar when it's time to reestablish contact with your school. If you are registering by mail, have the materials ready a few days in advance. You will probably discover that your vacation has provided exactly the respite you needed. Now you can resume work with the same zest as when you first began.

Twelve

After Graduation— What?

The Greek scientist Archimedes observed that even the greatest distance can be covered in tiny steps, provided you take enough of them. Every year, thousands of college returnees demonstrate that he was right. Hour by hour, credit by credit, they complete their course work and earn the degree.

Ask these graduates what difference college has made, and they barely know where to begin. A few have trouble remembering the time before they returned, not because it was so far back but because it has been obliterated by the crowded, eventful years at school.

Among traditional students, many mention the friends they have made. This is seldom a primary reason for pursuing the degree—there are certainly less taxing ways to achieve the same goal—but in the college classroom, with its informal atmosphere and shared interests, friendships are all but inevitable. One graduate estimates that of her closest friends, nearly half are people she met at school. "We do everything together," she notes. "We go out together, we eat together, our children have sleep-overs at each other's houses. I can't believe I didn't even know them three years ago!"

Careers are given high priority. Ours is a work-oriented society; jobs provide not only income but a large measure of identity and status. A newly licensed teacher takes over a fourth-grade class at the school where she had formerly been a paraprofessional. "I'm working twice as hard," she admits, "but this is my class, my kids. When they learn, it means we're all doing something right." A former supermarket clerk marvels that with his new degree in construction technology, he has already had two job offers and expects still more. One study of adults graduating from college showed that over half changed to a better job, 58 percent reported a promotion or salary increase, 64 percent received an increase in job responsibilities, and 76 percent noted an increase in status or respect from employers and co-workers.

As important as one's major field is the vast amount of background learning that takes place. Graduates are not always the best judges of how much they have learned; in some cases they assimilate the material so completely, they tend to feel it has always been part of them. John is quick to tell you that he has always loved opera; but in plain truth he has to admit that he never heard one, beginning to end, until he took required music. College may be where you first hear about genes, about Malthus, cuneiform writing, Gresham's law, Pushkin, geological faults, Madame Bovary, lemmings, sine curves, and a thousand other subjects. Students know that in most fields they have barely skimmed the surface, but they have made a start. They will add to it for the rest of their lives.

The most significant change is also the most elusive. "I'm a different person. I think differently."

College graduates are the first to admit that even in their own fields, they are very far from the frontiers of learning. But they know that the frontiers exist, and that scholars are working there to expand knowledge, as they have been for thousands of years. In each field research raises some questions even as it answers others; in time the questions give rise to new fields. The world becomes simultaneously more complex and more comprehensible. A flock of birds can be understood in terms of biology, aerodynamics, anatomy, ecology, music, art, social organization, or all at once. "I don't know anything," one graduate will tell you, "but I know how much there is to know."

Perspectives change; proportions change. Returnees are not

saints; you are still furious when someone at work gets the promotion you thought was coming to you. But at the same time, you know this is a small event in a very large world.

You have changed in still another way. Back when you first returned to college, you were not sure you could make it. Now you know. Somehow, you sustained the effort, the interest, the sheer dogged determination, to hang in until graduation. In that complex, exciting world of learning, you earned a corner for yourself.

Where do you go from here?

For the first time in years, you have a little extra time and money. Let's hope you have a bang-up celebration, an extended trip, or even a belated honeymoon. Just spending three successive weekends getting the garden into shape may be a luxury after budgeting every minute of your days and nights. One graduate is catching up on a three-year backlog of movies he missed the first time around. Another has indulged herself in a computerized chess game. More than a few decide it's time to start a family.

Perhaps this is the time to consolidate your gains. If you are starting a new job, you will want a chance to settle in; you will need to integrate the content of your courses with the realities of the workplace. You may need a breather to sort out all the ideas, facts, and points of view you have encountered over the past few years. You can extend your learning on your own. Did you read three Shakespeare plays in college? Look into the other thirty-five. If oceanography fascinated you, keep up with it through some of the readable new science magazines. You're free; you can do whatever you like.

Perhaps, though, you are not as elated as you think you ought to be. You have the degree, you can relax at last, but there is a sense of loss. The regimen of courses, credits, assignments, and reports wore you out and you couldn't wait to finish—but you miss it. The things you gave up were not really sacrifices; they were trade-offs. For everything you relinquished, you received something of greater value.

You are thinking of going back.

In her definitive study, *Adults as Learners* (1981), Patricia Cross writes,

Virtually all surveys, past and present, show that the more education people have, the more interested they will be in fur-

ther education, the more they will know about available opportunities, and the more they will participate. In short,
learning is addictive; the more education people have, the
more they want and the more they will get.

She's right. You're hooked.

There are, of course, many ways to learn. If you work well on
your own, you can simply set yourself a project of organized reading on a subject of interest. You can allow yourself the luxury of a
no-credit continuing education course, where the only pressures
are those you put on yourself. You can attend lectures and participate in archaeological digs.

Or you can return more formally for additional study—perhaps even for the next degree.

It will be easier this time. As you progress from one academic
level to the next, you concentrate on the fields of specific interest to
you, so your motivation and enthusiasm remain fresh. Your classmates will be increasingly sympathetic and your professors increasingly accessible. You can proceed at a leisurely pace; if this first
degree was a necessity, the next one may be a luxury. You've already proved that you can do it. And it doesn't matter whether you
are young or old. Only a handful of students move without inter-
ruption from high school to college to graduate work. Everyone
else drops back in.

Today the most remarkable thing about dropping back in is
that it is no longer remarkable. Your children may find it amusing
that you are a student again; the next generation will take it for
granted. Adults move easily from work to school and back again, in
channels created by the colleges themselves. The revolution is over.
You've won—and you're still winning.

Appendix 1

Statewide Agencies for Occupational and Professional Licensing

ALABAMA
Alabama Occupational
   Information Coordinating
   Committee
State Dept. of Education
First Southern Towers, Suite
   402
1100 Commerce Street
Montgomery 36130

ALASKA
Division of Occupational
   Licensing
Dept. of Commerce and
   Economic Development
Pouch D
Juneau 99811

ARIZONA
State Occupational Information
   Coordinating Committee
1535 W. Jefferson, Room 345
Phoenix 85007

ARKANSAS
Arkansas State Occupational
   Information Coordinating
   Committee
P.O. Box 5162
Little Rock 72205

CALIFORNIA
Dept. of Consumer Affairs
State and Consumer Services
   Agency
1020 N Street
Sacramento 95814

COLORADO
Dept. of Regulatory Agencies
Room 116, 1525 Sherman Street
Denver 80203

CONNECTICUT
Connecticut State Occupational
    Information Coordinating
    Committee
c/o Elm Street School
569 Maple Hill Avenue
Newington 06111

DELAWARE
Division of Business and Occu-
    pational Regulation
Dept. of Administrative Services
O'Neill Building
Dover 19901

DISTRICT OF COLUMBIA
Dept. of Licenses, Investigations
    and Inspections
605 G Street, NW
Washington 20001

FLORIDA
Dept. of Professional and Occu-
    pational Regulation
2009 Apalachee Parkway
Tallahassee 32301

GEORGIA
State Examining Boards
Office of Secretary of State
166 Pryor Street, SW
Atlanta 30334

HAWAII
Professional and Vocational Li-
    censing Division
Dept. of Regulatory Agencies
1010 Richards Street
Honolulu 96813

IDAHO
Bureau of Occupational Li-
    censes
Dept. of Self-Governing
    Agencies
2404 Bank Drive, Room 312
Boise 83705

ILLINOIS
Dept. of Registration and
    Education
320 W. Washington Street
Springfield 62786

INDIANA
Indiana Occupational
    Information Coordinating
    Committee
17 W. Market Street
434 Illinois Building
Indianapolis 46204

IOWA
Director of
Licensing and Certification
Dept. of Health
418 Sixth Avenue
Des Moines 50319

KANSAS
Kansas Occupational Informa-
    tion Coordinating Commit-
    tee
634 S. Harrrison, Suite C
Topeka 66603

KENTUCKY
Division of Occupations and
    Professions
Bureau of Administrative
    Services
Dept. of Finance
Twilight Trail, Building A
Frankfort 40601

LOUISIANA
Louisiana State Occupational
    Information Coordinating
    Committee
P.O. Box 44094
Baton Rouge 70804

MAINE
Central Licensing Division
Dept. of Business Regulation
Stevens School, State House
Augusta 04333

MARYLAND
HEALTH-RELATED:
Dept. of Health and Mental
    Hygiene
201 W. Preston Street
Baltimore 21201

OTHER:
Dept. of Licensing and
    Regulation
1 S. Calvert Street
Baltimore 21202

MASSACHUSETTS
Division of Registration
Office of Consumer Affairs
100 Cambridge Street
Boston 02202

MICHIGAN
Dept. of Licensing and
    Regulation
320 N. Washington
P.O. Box 30018
Lansing 48909

MINNESOTA
State Occupational Information
    Coordinating Committee
Dept. of Economic Security
690 American Center Building
150 E. Kellogg Boulevard
St. Paul 55010

MISSISSIPPI
State Occupational Information
    Coordinating Committee
Vocational Technical Education
P.O. Box 771
Jackson 39205

MISSOURI
Division of Professional
    Registration
Dept. of Consumer Affairs, Reg-
    ulation and Licensing
P.O. Box 1335
Jefferson City 65102

MONTANA
Dept. of Professional and Occu-
    pational Licensing
42½ N. Last Chance Gulch
Helena 59601

NEBRASKA
State Occupational Information
    Coordinating Committee
W. 300 Nebraska Hall
University of Nebraska
Lincoln 68588

NEVADA
State Occupational Information
    Coordinating Committee
Capitol Complex
505 E. King Street
Kinkead Building, Room 603
Carson City 89710

NEW HAMPSHIRE
State Occupational Information
    Coordinating Committee
Dept. of Employment Security
32 S. Main Street
Concord 03301

NEW JERSEY
Division of Consumer Affairs
Dept. of Law and Public Safety
1100 Raymond Boulevard
Newark 07102

NEW MEXICO
New Mexico State Occupational
   Information Coordinating
   Committee
Executive Plaza
4135-B Montgomery Boulevard,
   NE
Albuquerque 87125

NEW YORK
Division of Professional Licens-
   ing Services
Dept. of Education
Cultural Education Center,
   Room 3021
Albany 12230

NORTH CAROLINA
Secretary of State
State Capitol
Raleigh 27611

NORTH DAKOTA
Licensing Dept.
Office of Attorney General
State Capitol, 1st Floor
Bismarck 58505

OHIO
Ohio Occupational Information
   Coordinating Committee
State Dept. Building
S-65 S. Front Street, Room
   904
Columbus 43215

OKLAHOMA
State Occupational Information
   Coordinating Committee
School of Occupational and
   Adult Education
Oklahoma State University
1515 W. 6th Street
Stillwater 74074

OREGON
Dept. of Human Resources
930 State Office Building
Portland 97201

PENNSYLVANIA
Bureau of Professional and Oc-
   cupational Affairs
Dept. of State
Transportation and Safety
   Building, Room 618
Harrisburg 17120

PUERTO RICO
Examiners' Board
61 Tanca Street
San Juan 00904

RHODE ISLAND
Dept. of Business Regulation
100 N. Main Street
Providence 02903

SOUTH CAROLINA
South Carolina Occupational
   Information Coordinating
   Committee
1550 Gadsden Street
Columbia 29202

SOUTH DAKOTA
Division of Professional and Oc-
   cupational Licensing
Dept. of Commerce and Con-
   sumer Affairs
State Capitol
Pierre 57501

TENNESSEE
Regulatory Boards
Dept. of Insurance
506 Capitol Hill Building
Nashville 37219

TEXAS
State Occupational Information
    Coordinating Committee
Texas Employment Commission
    Building
15th and Congress, Room 648
Austin 78778

UTAH
Registration Division
Dept. of Business Regulation
330 E. Fourth South Street
Salt Lake City 84111

VERMONT
Division of Licensing and
    Regulation
Office of Secretary of State
Pavilion Office Building
Montpelier 05602

VIRGINIA
Dept. of Commerce
2 S. Ninth Street
Richmond 23219

WASHINGTON
Dept. of Licensing
Highways-Licenses Building
Olympia 98504

WEST VIRGINIA
State Occupational Information
    Coordinating Committee
1600½ Washington Street, E
Charleston 25305

WISCONSIN
Dept. of Regulation and
    Licensing
1400 E. Washington Avenue
Madison 53702

WYOMING
Wyoming Occupational
    Information Coordinating
    Committee
Hathaway Building
2300 Capitol Avenue
Cheyenne 82002

Appendix 2

Professional Accrediting Agencies

ALLIED HEALTH: See
MEDICAL ASSISTANT,
MEDICAL TECHNOL-
OGY,
PUBLIC HEALTH

ARCHITECTURE
National Architectural Accrediting Board
1735 New York Avenue, NW
Washington, DC 20006

ART
National Association of Schools
of Art
Commission on Accreditation
11250 Roger Bacon Drive,
Suite 5
Reston, VA 22090

BIBLE COLLEGE
EDUCATION
American Association of Bible
Colleges
Box 1523
130-F N. College Street
Fayetteville, AR 72701

BUSINESS
American Assembly of Collegiate Schools of Business
11500 Olive Street Road, Suite
142
St. Louis, MO 63141

CHEMISTRY
American Chemical Society
Committee on Professional
Training
1155 Sixteenth Street, NW
Washington, DC 20036

CHIROPRACTIC
EDUCATION
The Council on Chiropractic
Education
3209 Ingersoll Avenue
Des Moines, IA 50312

CLINICAL PASTORAL
EDUCATION
Association for Clinical Pastoral
Education, Inc.
Interchurch Center, Suite 450
475 Riverside Drive
New York, NY 10027

CONSTRUCTION
EDUCATION
American Council for
Construction Education
P.O. Box 1266
103 S. Fourth Street, Suite 6
Manhattan, KS 66502

DENTISTRY AND DENTAL
AUXILIARY PROGRAMS
American Dental Association
Commission on Dental
Accreditation
211 E. Chicago Avenue
Chicago, IL 60611

DIETETICS
The American Dietetic
Association
Commission on Accreditation
430 N. Michigan Avenue
Chicago, IL 60611

ENGINEERING
Accreditation Board for Engineering and Technology
345 East 47th Street
New York, NY 10017

FORESTRY
Society of American Foresters
5400 Grosvenor Lane
Washington, DC 20014

FUNERAL SERVICE
EDUCATION
American Board of Funeral Ser-
vice Education
Box 2098
Fairmont, WV 26554

HEALTH SERVICES
ADMINISTRATION
GRADUATE PROGRAMS:
Accrediting Commission on
Education for Health Ser-
vices Administration
1 Dupont Circle, NW, Suite
420
Washington, DC 20036
See also *MEDICAL
TECHNOLOGY*

HOME ECONOMICS
American Home Economics
Association
Office of Professional Education
2010 Massachusetts Avenue,
NW
Washington, DC 20036

INDUSTRIAL TECHNOLOGY
National Association for Indus-
trial Technology
University of North Florida
Division of Technologies
P.O. Box 17074
Jacksonville, FL 32216

INTERIOR DESIGN
Foundation for Interior Design
Education Research
730 Fifth Avenue
New York, NY 10019

JOURNALISM
American Council on Education
for Journalism
Accrediting Committee
563 Essex Court
Deerfield, IL 60015

LANDSCAPE
ARCHITECTURE
Amerian Society of Landscape
Architects
Landscape Architectural
Accreditation Board
1900 M Street, NW,
Suite 750
Washington, DC 20036

LAW
American Bar Association
Indianapolis Law School
Indiana University–Purdue
University at Indianapolis
735 W. New York Street
Indianapolis, IN 46202

LIBRARIANSHIP
American Library Association
Committee on Accreditation
50 E. Huron Street
Chicago, IL 60611

MEDICAL ASSISTANT/
MEDICAL LABORATORY
TECHNICIAN
DIPLOMA, CERTIFICATE, AND AS-
SOCIATE'S DEGREE PRO-
GRAMS:
Accrediting Bureau of Health
Education Schools
Oak Manor Offices
29089 U.S. 20 West
Elkhart, IN 46514

MEDICAL TECHNOLOGY
American Medical Association
Dept. of Allied Health Educa-
tion and Accreditation
535 North Dearborn Street
Chicago, IL 60610
Covers the following areas:
Blood-Bank Technology, Car-
diovascular Perfusionist, Cy-
totechnologist, Diagnostic
Medical Sonographer, EEG
Technologist, EMT-Paramed-
ic, Histologic Technician,
Laboratory Assistant, Medical
Assistant, Medical Assistant in
Pediatrics, Medical Labora-
tory Technician, Medical
Record Administrator, Medi-
cal Record Technician, Medi-
cal Technologist, Nuclear
Medicine Technologist, Occupational Therapist, Operating
Room Technician, Ophthal-
mic Medical Assistant, Physical Therapist, Physician's Assistant, Radiation Therapy
Technologist, Radiologic
Technician, Respiratory
Therapist, Respiratory Therapy Technician, Surgeon's Assistant, Surgical Technologist

MEDICINE
ODD-NUMBERED YEARS, BEGIN-
NING EACH JULY:
Council on Medical Education
American Medical Association
535 N. Dearborn Street
Chicago, IL 60610

EVEN-NUMBERED YEARS, BEGIN-
NING EACH JULY:
Association of American Medi-
cal Colleges
1 Dupont Circle, NW, Suite 200
Washington, DC 20036

MUSIC
National Association of Schools
of Music
11250 Roger Bacon Drive, No. 5
Reston, VA 22090

NURSING
PRACTICAL NURSING ONLY:
National Association for Practi-
cal Nurse Education and
Service
122 East 42nd Street, Suite 800
New York, NY 10017

OTHER:
National League for Nursing
10 Columbus Circle
New York, NY 10019

OCCUPATIONAL, TRADE,
AND TECHNICAL
EDUCATION
National Association of Trade
and Technical Schools
2021 K Street, NW
Washington, DC 20006

OPTOMETRY
American Optometric
Association
Council on Optometric
Education
243 N. Lindbergh Boulevard
St. Louis, MO 63141

OSTEOPATHIC MEDICINE
American Osteopathic
Association
Bureau of Professional Educa-
tion
212 E. Ohio Street
Chicago, IL 60611

PARAMEDICAL FIELDS: See
*MEDICAL TECHNOL-
OGY, PUBLIC HEALTH*

PHARMACY
American Council on Pharma-
ceutical Education
1 E. Wacker Drive
Chicago, IL 60601

PHYSICAL THERAPY
American Physical Therapy
Association
Dept. of Educational Affairs
1156 Fifteenth Street, NW
Washington, DC 20005

PODIATRY
American Podiatry Association
Council on Podiatry Education
20 Chevy Chase Circle, NW
Washington, DC 20015

PSYCHOLOGY
American Psychological
Association
1200 Seventeenth Street, NW
Washington, DC 20036

PUBLIC HEALTH
Council on Education for Public
Health
1015 Fifteenth Street, NW,
Suite 403
Washington, DC 20005

RABBINICAL AND TAL-
MUDIC EDUCATION
Association of Advanced Rab-
binical and Talmudic
Schools
175 Fifth Avenue
New York, NY 10010

REHABILITATION
    COUNSELING
Council on Rehabilitation
    Education
3101 S. Dearborn Street, Room
    246C
Chicago, IL 60616

SOCIAL WORK
Council on Social Work
    Education
Education Standards and
    Accreditation
111 Eighth Avenue, Suite 501
New York, NY 10011

SPEECH PATHOLOGY AND
    AUDIOLOGY
American Speech, Language,
    and Hearing Association
Office of Education and Scien-
    tific Programs
10801 Rockville Pike
Rockville, MD 20852

TEACHER EDUCATION
National Council for Accredita-
    tion of Teacher Education
1919 Pennsylvania Avenue,
    NW, Suite 202
Washington, DC 20006

THEOLOGY
Association of Theological
    Schools in the United
    States and Canada
42 E. National Road
P.O. Box 130
Vandalia, OH 45377

VETERINARY MEDICINE
American Veterinary Medical
    Association
Office of Scientific Activities
930 N. Meacham Road
Schaumburg, IL 60196

Appendix 3

Statewide Agencies for Higher Education

(Separate agencies for two-year colleges are listed when indicated; otherwise, use the given address.)

ALABAMA

TWO-YEAR COLLEGES:
Alabama State Dept. of
    Education
Postsecondary Division
817 S. Court Street
Montgomery 36104
(205) 832-3340

OTHER:
Alabama Commission on
    Higher Education
1 Court Square, Suite
    221
Montgomery 36197
(205) 832-6555

ALASKA

TWO-YEAR COLLEGES:
Division of Community Colleges, Rural Education, and
    Extension
University of Alaska
2221 E. Northern Lights Boulevard, No. 137
Anchorage 99504
(907) 274-0548

OTHER:
Alaska Commission on Postsecondary Education
Pouch F, State Office Building
Juneau 99811
(907) 465-2854

ARIZONA
TWO-YEAR COLLEGES:
State Board of Directors for
 Community Colleges of
 Arizona
Building A
1937 W. Jefferson, Suite 123
Phoenix 85009
(602) 255-4037

OTHER:
State Board of Regents
1535 W. Jefferson, Suite 121
Phoenix 85007
(602) 255-4082

ARKANSAS
Dept. of Higher Education
1301 West 7th Street
Little Rock 72201
(501) 371-1441

CALIFORNIA
TWO-YEAR COLLEGES:
Board of Governors of California Community Colleges
1238 S Street
Sacramento 95814
(916) 322-4005

OTHER:
California Postsecondary Education Commission
1020 12th Street
Sacramento 95814
(916) 445-1000

COLORADO
TWO-YEAR COLLEGES:
State Board for Community
 Colleges and Occupational
 Education
221 Centennial Building, 2nd
 Floor
1313 Sherman Street
Denver 80203
(303) 839-3151

OTHER:
Colorado Commission on
 Higher Education
1550 Lincoln Street
Denver 80203
(303) 839-2723

CONNECTICUT
TWO-YEAR COLLEGES:
Regional Community Colleges
61 Woodland Street
Hartford 06105
(203) 566-8760

OTHER:
State Board of Higher Education
61 Woodland Street
Hartford 06105
(203) 566-3913

DELAWARE
TWO-YEAR COLLEGES:
Delaware Technical and Com-
 munity College
P.O. Box 897
Dover 19901
(302) 736-4621

OTHER:
Delaware Postsecondary Education Commission
1228 N. Scott Street, Suite 1
Wilmington 19806
(302) 571-3240

NOTE: For University of Delaware, write directly to the
 university.

DISTRICT OF COLUMBIA
District of Columbia Commission on Postsecondary
 Education
421 8th Street, NW, Room 206
Washington 20004
(202) 727-3685

FLORIDA

TWO-YEAR COLLEGES:
Florida Dept. of Education
Division of Community Colleges
310 Collins Building
Tallahassee 32301
(904) 488-1721

OTHER:
Florida Dept. of Education
W. V. Knott Building
Tallahassee 32301
(904) 488-0816

GEORGIA

Board of Regents of the University System of Georgia
244 Washington Street, SW
Atlanta 30334
TWO-YEAR COLLEGES: (404) 656-2213
OTHER: (404) 656-2202

HAWAII

TWO-YEAR COLLEGES:
University of Hawaii
Dole Street Offices
2327 Dole Street
Honolulu 96822
(808) 948-7313

OTHER:
University of Hawaii
Bachman Hall
2444 Dole Street
Honolulu 96822
(808) 948-8207

IDAHO:

State Board of Education and Board of Regents of the University of Idaho
650 W. State Street
Boise 83720
(208) 334-2270

ILLINOIS

TWO-YEAR COLLEGES:
Illinois Community College Board
3085 Stevenson Drive
Springfield 62703
(217) 786-6000

OTHER:
Illinois Board of Higher Education
4 W. Old Capitol Square
500 Reisch Building
Springfield 62701
(217) 782-2551

INDIANA

Indiana Commission for Higher Education
143 W. Market Street
Indianapolis 46204
(317) 232-1900

IOWA

TWO-YEAR COLLEGES:
Iowa State Board of Public Instruction
Grimes State Office Building
Des Moines 50319
(515) 281-5294

OTHER:
Iowa State Board of Regents
Lucas State Office Building
Des Moines 50319
(515) 281-3934

KANSAS

TWO-YEAR COLLEGES:
State Dept. of Education
Postsecondary Administration Section, Community College Unit
120 E. 10th Street
Topeka 66612
(913) 296-3047

OTHER:
Board of Regents, State of Kansas
Merchants National Bank
Tower
Topeka 66612
(913) 296-3421

KENTUCKY
TWO-YEAR COLLEGES:
University of Kentucky
102 Breckinridge Hall
Lexington 40506
(606) 258-8607

OTHER:
Council on Higher Education
West Frankfort Office Complex
Frankfort 40601
(502) 564-3553

LOUISIANA
Louisiana Board of Regents
1 American Place, Suite 1530
Baton Rouge 70825
(504) 342-4253

MAINE
University of Maine Board of
Trustees
107 Maine Avenue
Bangor 04401
(207) 947-0336

MARYLAND
TWO-YEAR COLLEGES:
Maryland State Board for Community Colleges
Jeffrey Building
16 Francis Street
Annapolis 21401
(301) 269-2881

OTHER:
Maryland State Board for
Higher Education
16 Francis Street
Annapolis 21401
(301) 269-2971

MASSACHUSETTS
TWO-YEAR COLLEGES:
Board of Regional Community
Colleges
470 Atlantic Avenue
Boston 02210
(617) 727-1260

OTHER:
Board of Higher Education
31 Saint James Avenue, Suite
323
Boston 02116
(617) 727-5360

MICHIGAN
State Board of Education
P.O. Box 30008
Lansing 48909
TWO-YEAR COLLEGES: (517) 373-
3820
OTHER: (517) 373-3354

MINNESOTA
TWO-YEAR COLLEGES:
Minnesota State Board for Community Colleges
301 Capitol Square
550 Cedar Street
St. Paul 55101
(612) 296-3356

OTHER:
Minnesota Higher Education
Coordinating Board
550 Cedar Street, Suite 400
St. Paul 55101
(612) 296-3974

MISSISSIPPI

TWO-YEAR COLLEGES:
State Dept. of Education
Division of Junior Colleges
P.O. Box 771
Jackson 39205
(601) 354-6962

OTHER:
Board of Trustees of State Institutions of Higher Learning
P.O. Box 2336
Jackson 39205
(601) 982-6611

MISSOURI

Coordinating Board for Higher
    Education
600 Monroe Avenue
Jefferson City 65101
(314) 751-2361

MONTANA

Montana Board of Regents of
    Higher Education
33 S. Last Chance Gulch
Helena 59601
(406) 449-3024

NEBRASKA

Nebraska Coordinating Commission for Postsecondary
    Education
301 Centennial Mall, S
P.O. Box 95005
Lincoln 68509
(402) 471-2847

NEVADA

Board of Regents, University of
    Nevada System
405 Marsh Avenue
Reno 89509
(702) 784-4901

NEW HAMPSHIRE

TWO-YEAR COLLEGES:
State Dept. of Education
Division of Postsecondary
    Education
163 Loudon Road
Concord 03301
(603) 271-2722

OTHER:
New Hampshire Postsecondary
    Education Commission
61 S. Spring Street
Concord 03301
(603) 271-2555

NEW JERSEY

State Board of Higher Education
225 W. State Street
Trenton 08625
TWO-YEAR COLLEGES: (609) 292-4470
OTHER: (609) 292-4310

NEW MEXICO

Board of Educational Finance
1068 Cerrillos Road
Santa Fe 87503
(505) 827-2115

NEW YORK

Regents of the University of the
    State of New York
State Education Department
Albany 12234
(518) 474-5889

NORTH CAROLINA

TWO-YEAR COLLEGES:
State Board of Education
Dept. of Community Colleges
Education Building, Room 194
116 W. Edenton Street
Raleigh 27611
(919) 733-7051

OTHER:
Board of Governors of the University of North Carolina
P.O. Box 2688
Chapel Hill 27514
(919) 933-6981

NORTH DAKOTA
North Dakota State Board of Higher Education
State Capitol Building
Bismarck 58505
(701) 224-2960

OHIO
Ohio Board of Regents
30 E. Broad Street
Columbus 43215
TWO-YEAR COLLEGES: (614) 466-5810
OTHER: (614) 466-6000

OKLAHOMA
Oklahoma State Regents for Higher Education
500 Education Building
State Capitol Complex
Oklahoma City 73105
(405) 521-2444

OREGON
TWO-YEAR COLLEGES:
Oregon Dept. of Education
Division of Community Colleges
700 Pringle Parkway, SE
Salem 97310
(503) 378-8609

OTHER:
Educational Coordinating Commission
495 State Street
Salem 97310
(503) 378-3921

PENNSYLVANIA
State Board of Education
333 Market Street
(Two-year colleges: add Box 911)
Harrisburg 17108
(717) 787-5041

PUERTO RICO
Council on Higher Education
Box F, UPR Station
San Juan 00931
(809) 765-6590

RHODE ISLAND
TWO-YEAR COLLEGES:
Community College of Rhode Island
400 East Avenue
Warwick 02886
(401) 825-2188

OTHER:
Board of Regents for Education
199 Promenade Street, Suite 208
Providence 02908
(401) 277-2031

SOUTH CAROLINA
TWO-YEAR COLLEGES:
State Board for Technical and Comprehensive Education
1429 Senate Street
Columbia 29201
(803) 758-3173

OTHER:
South Carolina Commission on Higher Education
1429 Senate Street, Suite 1104
Columbia 29201
(803) 758-2407

SOUTH DAKOTA
South Dakota Board of Regents;
   Dept. of Educational and
   Cultural Affairs
Kneip Office Building
Pierre 57501
(605) 773-3455

TENNESSEE
TWO-YEAR COLLEGES:
State Board of Regents (State
   University and Community
   College System of
   Tennessee)
1161 Murfreesboro Road
Nashville 37217
(615) 741-4821

OTHER:
Tennessee Higher Education
   Commission
501 Union Building, Suite 300
Nashville 37219
(615) 741-3605

TEXAS
Coordinating Board, Texas Col-
   lege and University System
P.O. Box 12788, Capitol Station
Austin 78711
TWO-YEAR COLLEGES: (512) 475-
   3413
OTHER: (512) 475-4361

UTAH
State Board of Regents
807 E. South Temple Street
Salt Lake City 84102
(801) 533-5617

VERMONT
Vermont State Colleges
P.O. Box 349
Waterbury 05676
(802) 244-7871

NOTE: For University of Vermont, write directly to the
   university.

VIRGINIA
TWO-YEAR COLLEGES:
Virginia Community College
   System
P.O. Box 1558
Richmond 23212
(804) 786-2231

OTHER:
State Council of Higher
   Education
700 Fidelity Building
Ninth and Main Streets
Richmond 23219
(804) 786-2143

WASHINGTON
TWO-YEAR COLLEGES:
State Board for Community
   College Education
319 Seventh Avenue
Olympia 98504
(206) 753-7412

OTHER:
Council for Postsecondary
   Education
908 E. Fifth Avenue
Olympia 98504
(206) 753-3241

WEST VIRGINIA
West Virginia Board of Regents
950 Kanawha Boulevard, E
Charleston 25301
(304) 348-2101

WISCONSIN

TWO-YEAR COLLEGES:

Wisconsin Board of Vocational, Technical, and Adult Education
4802 Sheboygan Avenue, 7th Floor
Madison 53702
(608) 266-1770

OTHER:

Board of Regents of the University of Wisconsin System
1860 Van Hise Hall
1220 Linden Drive
Madison 53706
(608) 262-2324

WYOMING

TWO-YEAR COLLEGES:

Wyoming Community College Commission
1720 Carey Avenue
Cheyenne 82001
(307) 777-7763

OTHER:

University of Wyoming Trustees
P.O. Box 3434, University Station
Laramie 82071
(307) 766-4121

Bibliography

ASLANIAN, CAROL B., and BRICKELL, HENRY M. *Americans in Transition: Life Changes as a Reason for Adult Learning.* New York: College Entrance Examination Board, 1978.

BERG, IVAR. *Education and Jobs.* Boston: Beacon Press, 1971.

BOYD, ROBERT D., and APPS, JEROLD. *Redefining the Discipline of Adult Education.* San Francisco: Jossey-Bass, 1980.

BOYER, ERNEST L., and LEVINE, ARTHUR. *A Quest for Common Learning.* Washington, D.C.: The Carnegie Foundation for the Advancement of Teaching, 1980.

BRUBACHER, JOHN S., and RUDY, WILLIS. *Higher Education in Transition.* New York: Harper & Row, 1976.

Carnegie Commission on Higher Education. *Less Time, More Options.* New York: McGraw-Hill, 1971.

CHICKERING, ARTHUR W., and Associates. *The Modern American College.* San Francisco: Jossey-Bass, 1981.

CLEP General and Subject Examinations. New York: The College Board, 1979.

College Blue Book: Degrees Offered by College and Subject. New York: The Macmillan Co., 1981.

College Handbook Index of Majors. New York: College Entrance Examination Board, 1981.

College Placement and Credit by Examination. New York: College Entrance Examination Board, 1978.

Credit by Examination Comes of Age. New York: College Entrance Examination Board, 1980.

CROSS, K. PATRICIA. *Adults as Learners.* San Francisco: Jossey-Bass, 1981.

————. *The Missing Link: Connecting Adult Learners to Learning Resources.* New York: The College Board, 1978.

————, VALLEY, JOHN R., and Associates. *Planning Non-Traditional Programs: An Analysis of the Issues for Post-Secondary Education.* San Francisco: Jossey-Bass, 1974.

CROSS, WILBUR. *The Weekend Education Source Book.* New York: Harper's Magazine Press, 1976.

CROSSLAND, FRED E. "Learning to Cope with a Downward Slope." *Change 12,* no. 5 (July–August 1980), 18–21.

DEARMAN, NANCY B., and PLISKO, VALENA W. *The Condition of Education, 1981 Edition.* Washington, D.C.: National Center for Educational Statistics, 1981.

DRESSEL, PAUL L., and THOMPSON, MARY M. *Independent Study.* San Francisco: Jossey-Bass, 1973.

EISENBERG, GERSON G. *Vacation Programs.* Baltimore, Md.: Eisenberg Educational Enterprises, 1980.

EKSTROM, RUTH B., HARRIS, ABIGAIL M., and LOCKHEED, MARLAINE E. *How to Get College Credit for What You Have Learned as a Homemaker and Volunteer.* Princeton, N.J.: Educational Testing Service, 1977.

Evaluative Look at Nontraditional Postsecondary Education, An. Washington, D.C.: The National Institute of Education, 1979.

GROSS, RONALD. *Higher/Wider Education.* New York: The Ford Foundation, 1976.

————. *The Lifelong Learner.* New York: Simon & Schuster, 1977.

Guide to Educational Programs in Noncollegiate Organizations, A. Albany, N.Y.: The University of the State of New York, 1980.

Guide to the Evaluation of Educational Experiences in the Armed Forces. Washington, D.C.: American Council on Education, 1980.

HARRIS, SHERRY S., ed. *1980–81 Accredited Institutions of Postsecondary Education.* Washington, D.C.: American Council on Education, 1980.

HARRINGTON, FRED HARVEY. *The Future of Higher Education.* San Francisco: Jossey-Bass, 1977.

HECHINGER, FRED. "About Education: Future for Colleges Is Painted Brighter." *The New York Times,* January 13, 1981, p. C4.

HOULE, CYRIL. *The External Degree.* San Francisco: Jossey-Bass, 1977.

HUNTER, JOAN H., ed. *Guide to Independent Study Through Correspondence Instruction 1980–1982.* Princeton, N.J.: Peterson's Guides, 1980.

KASWORM, CAROL E. "The Older Student as an Undergraduate." *Adult Education* 31, no. 1 (Fall 1980), 30–47.

KEATON, MORRIS, ed. *Experiential Learning: Rationale, Characteristics and Assessment.* San Francisco: Jossey-Bass, 1976.

LENZ, ELINOR, and SHAEVITZ, MARJORIE HANSEN. *So You Want to Go Back to College.* New York: McGraw-Hill, 1977.

MAXWELL, MARTHA. *Improving Student Learning Skills.* San Francisco: Jossey-Bass, 1979.

MENDELSOHN, PAM. *Happier by Degrees.* New York: E.P. Dutton, 1980.

MEYER, PETER. *Awarding College Credit for Non-College Learning.* San Francisco: Jossey-Bass, 1975.

MINCER, JACOB. *Schooling, Experience, and Earnings.* New York: National Bureau of Economic Research, 1974.

National Guide to Credit Recommendations for Non-Collegiate Courses. Washington, D.C.: American Council on Education, 1979.

Occupational Outlook for College Graduates. Washington, D.C.: U.S. Department of Labor, 1980.

Paying for Your Education: A Guide for Adult Learners. New York: College Entrance Examination Board, 1980.

PETERSON, RICHARD E., and Associates. *Lifelong Learning in America.* San Francisco: Jossey-Bass, 1979.

Regents External Degrees: College Proficiency Examinations. Albany, N.Y.: The University of the State of New York, 1980.

Regional Directories of Institutions Awarding Credit for Noncollegiate Learning. Columbia, Md.: Council for the Advancement of Experiential Learning (CAEL), 1981.

SOSDIAN, CAROL P., and SHARP, LAURE M. *The External Degree as a Credential.* Washington, D.C.: National Institute of Education, 1978.

State Administrative Officials Classified by Function. Lexington, Ky.: The Council of State Governments, 1979.

TRILLIN, ALICE, and Associates. *Teaching Basic Skills in College.* San Francisco: Jossey-Bass, 1980.

Undergraduate Programs of Cooperative Education in the United States. Boston: National Commission for Cooperative Education, 1980.

Who Offers Part-Time Degree Programs? Princeton, N.J.: Peterson's Guides, 1981.

Index

MIRIAM HECHT spent the first ten years of her professional life as a writer. She returned to college after the birth of her two children, earning degrees in mathematics and mathematics education. She is currently a professor at Hunter College in New York, where she works extensively with returning adults.

LILLIAN TRAUB, the mother of three, dropped back into college after twenty years in advertising to obtain an M.A. degree as a vocational counselor of adults. She has worked with the New York Employment Service, the San Diego Department of Education, and on projects ranging from vocational rehabilitation of the disabled to counseling and placement for homemakers returning to the job market. She is now a vocational and educational consultant for adults in the Los Angeles area.

MORE CAREER GUIDANCE BOOKS FROM DUTTON

BLUE-COLLAR JOBS FOR WOMEN
by Muriel Lederer

A comprehensive guide for women that tells how to get skilled and get a high-paying job in the trades.
$7.95, paperback   ISBN: 0-87690-319-7

THE COMPLETE PHOTOGRAPHY CAREERS HANDBOOK
by George Gilbert

A thorough and well-organized handbook of educational and career opportunities in the field of photography.
$15.95, cloth   ISBN: 0-525-93238-0
$7.95, paperback   ISBN: 0-525-93237-2

HAPPIER BY DEGREES
by Pam Mendelsohn

A comprehensive guide for women considering going back to school.
$7.95, paperback   ISBN: 0-525-93085-X

HOW TO GET INTO LAW SCHOOL
by Rennard Strickland

An inside look at the law school admissions process.
$4.95, paperback   ISBN: 0-8015-3767-3

HOW TO GET INTO MEDICAL SCHOOL
by Marvin Fogel and Mort Walker

A comprehensive guide for the student making application to medical school.
$7.25, paperback   ISBN: 0-8015-3670-7

HOW TO GET THE JOB YOU WANT IN 28 DAYS
by Tom Jackson

How to launch and successfully complete a well-focused and rewarding job search.
$9.25, paperback   ISBN: 0-8015-9202-X

HOW TO PUT YOUR BOOK TOGETHER AND GET A JOB IN ADVERTISING
by Maxine Paetro

Step-by-step demonstrations for compiling an ad portfolio for the job hunt.
$7.95, paperback   ISBN: 0-8015-3748-7

IN FRONT OF THE CAMERA
by Bernard Sandler with Steve Posner

Inside advice on how to build and maintain a career in the movies and television.

$13.50, cloth	ISBN: 0-525-93176-7
$8.25, paperback	ISBN: 0-525-93177-5

INSIDE THE LAW SCHOOLS
by Sally F. Goldfarb

Current law students report on faculty, social life, and prestige of their schools, including advice on law boards, grades, interviews, and applications.

$9.25, paperback   ISBN: 0-525-93243-7

THE STUDENT GUIDE TO FELLOWSHIPS AND INTERNSHIPS
by the Students of Amherst College

Hundreds of listings with comprehensive explanations of positions in every field.

$15.95, cloth	ISBN: 0-525-93155-4
$7.95, paperback	ISBN: 0-525-93147-3

THE WHOLE WORLD HANDBOOK
by the Council on International Educational Exchange

A guide to study, work, and travel abroad.

$5.75, paperback   ISBN: 0-525-93171-6

Available at bookstores or from E.P. Dutton. To order from Dutton, list titles and ISBN numbers. Send a check or money order for the retail price plus appropriate sales tax and 10% for postage and handling to Dept. CW, E.P. Dutton, 2 Park Avenue, New York, NY 10016. New York residents must add sales tax. Allow up to six weeks for delivery.